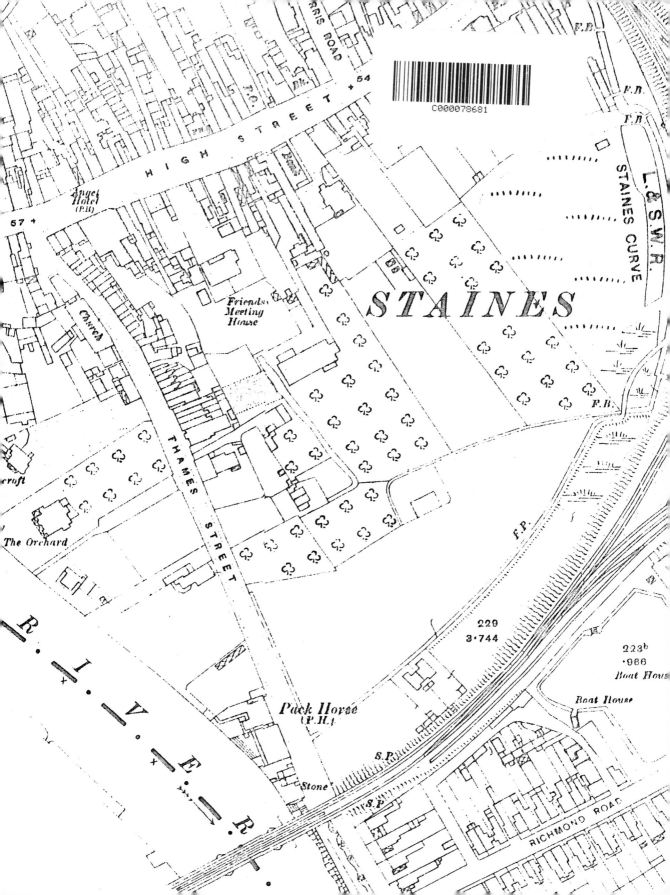

STAINES
A History

Staines Bridge, 1949. The emergency bridge, built in the Second World War, demonstrates how vital the river crossing remained for 2,000 years. In the foreground is the Lagonda car works.

STAINES
A History

Pamela Maryfield

Phillimore

2006

Published by
PHILLIMORE & CO. LTD
Shopwyke Manor Barn, Chichester, West Sussex, England
www.phillimore.co.uk

ISBN 1-86077-420-2
ISBN 13 978-1-86077-420-1

Printed and bound in Great Britain by
CROMWELL PRESS LTD
Trowbridge, Wiltshire

CONTENTS

LIST OF ILLUSTRATIONS

ACKNOWLEDGEMENTS

I would like to thank the staff who have helped me with such skill and patience at the Surrey History Centre, the London Metropolitan Archives and the National Archives. Margaret White, chairman of the Egham-by-Runnymede Historical Society, has shared her wide knowledge of the society's picture resources. Other members who, week by week, keep the museum open and active, have invariably made me welcome and answered my queries. Joan Gardam was a generous and knowledgeable guide to aspects of Staines that I would have taken too long to discover. (My dog now enjoys the Moor.) Vivian Bairstow kindly gave permission on behalf of the Egham Museum Trust for me to use a large number of pictures – almost one-third of the book's total – from the museum's collection and plugged gaps from his own. I am grateful for the loan of a substantial number of illustrations from Graham Dennis's collection and for Jeremy Smith of Guildhall Library ensuring a high quality of image and answering my numerous enquiries.

Illustration Acknowledgements

Vivian Bairstow: 48, 92, 98, 102, 103, 107
Chertsey Museum: 22, 23
Claydon House Trust: 52, 58
Graham Dennis Collection: 10, 12, 13, 14, 15, 53, 55, 61, 71, 77, 86, 90, 94, 95, 96
Dewguard, Egham: 101
Egham Museum Collection: frontispiece, 1, 4, 7, 17, 18, 19, 24, 26, 27, 28, 35, 56, 67, 68, 69, 73, 74, 79, 83, 87, 88, 89, 92, 93, 104, 105, 106
Chris Gardam ©: 57, 108
Guildhall Art Gallery, Corporation of London: 31
Guildhall Library, City of London: 3, 11, 29, 49, 54, 76, 77, 80, 81
London Metropolitan Archives: 36, 37, 46, 47, 59, 62, 72, 75
Council for British Archaeology and Phillipa Bradley: 5
The National Archives: 21, 42, 43, 44, 45, 51
National Monuments Record: 34, 38, 39
Phillimore & Co. Ltd: 9, 20
Royal Collection ©: 2006 Her Majesty Queen Elizabeth II: 32, 78
Reproduced by permission of Surrey History Service: 50, 53, 54, 60, 63, 64, 66, 85, 91, 97, 99, 100

F. Turner: 33, 40
Westminster Abbey Muniments & Library (Copyright: Dean and Chapter of Westminster):
    15, 16
Richard Williams ©: 2
The Author: Cover Picture, 6, 8, 25, 30, 41, 65, 82, 84

Chapter One

ORIGINS: ROMANS, SAXONS AND VIKINGS

Staines owes its strategic position at a Thames crossing as much to geology as to geography. The Romans recognised the site's special characteristics and chose it for the bridge to carry the early primary route from Silchester (Calleva Atrebatum) over the Thames and onwards to London or Colchester (Camulodunum). It was called Pontes and was referred to in the locative case (Pontibus) in the third-century Antonine Itinerary. From the repeated use of the plural, we know that there was more than one bridge. A second may have been constructed over the River Colne just to the west.

Staines' geological advantage was the presence of islands of gravel on either bank of the Thames to provide the firm footings for a bridge. The southern bank consists of an almost continuous stretch of alluvium upstream from Hampton and was liable to annual flooding. On the north bank, the complex river system, formed by the River Colne and its channels, created a marshy area unsuitable for a road or the footings of a major bridge. This whole area is hard to imagine as it was. Today the M25, a complex motorway junction, a string of gravel pits and large reservoirs largely cover it. But the flooding needs no leap of the imagination for residents who can recall the floods of 1947 and 1953.

The settlements of Staines and Laleham lie on patches of brickearth and gravel between 25 and 75 feet above sea level. There is a continuation of a brickearth outcrop east of the core Roman settlement along the line of the A30. North and south there are alluvial outcrops. In fact, Staines was a cluster of small settlements on gravel islands surrounded by land subject to annual flooding. Stretching north from the site of St Mary's Church is a promontory of gravel above the 50-foot contour, bounded by the River Wyrardisbury and the old county boundary known as the Shire ditch. This was the site of a prehistoric (Neolithic) causewayed enclosure at Yeoveney.

However, signs of earlier human activity have been found. From Church Lammas, distinctive long blade flints have been excavated, dating from the Upper Palaeolithic (*c.*8000 BC). They are evidence of a long-distance trade. The same type has been found in France at Belloy-sur-Somme, at Three Ways Wharf, Uxbridge and may originate at the Ahrensburg site in northern Germany.

Mesolithic activity is represented by knapped flint tranchets, five to six inches long and skilfully shaped to fit into the hand. Red deer antlers were used as adzes. Both sets of implements probably represent industrial activity. A site at 10-16 London Road, Staines has revealed Mesolithic pits.

The Yeoveney enclosure represents new technologies and a more settled agricultural mode of life, with stock-rearing of cattle,

1 River Thames *c*.1950 looking east across Longmead towards Runnymede. Egham is on the higher ground and in the distant top left is the Thames crossing. The tree line, right, marks one of the possible old courses of the river.

pigs and sheep. It belongs to a form of Neolithic structure that is widespread throughout Europe and has many examples in Wessex. Windmill Hill at Avebury and Maiden Castle in Dorset are typical. These structures were not for defence nor permanently occupied. Yeoveney would have been inaccessible for large parts of each year. Locally it was probably associated with a rich scatter of ritual monuments, a cursus of four kilometres and henges, on the Heathrow plateau. It had two concentric ditches with several gaps for entry to the central area. The ditches were 20 metres apart. It was roughly circular with a flattened 'side' to the south-east. Philippa Bradley argues strongly for its ritual purpose. Pottery shards (5,000 representing almost 1,500 vessels), struck flints and bones, some human, were distributed ritually and deliberately on the site.

While current interpretation of sites such as Yeoveney leans towards their ritual function, they may also have had another practical purpose, that of gathering the cattle in early autumn to determine which should be over-wintered for breeding and which should be slaughtered. Widespread finds of scrapers used to clean and prepare skins provide support for this view.

Within the area of the modern town centre recent excavations show considerable prehistoric activity. One of these is the site at the Friends Burial Ground, where there were two Neolithic pits and worked flints. On Runnymede, across the river, signs of a rectangular 'long house' and middens may be associated with the Yeoveney site.

Gradually a rich collection of archaeological evidence is revealing substantial activity and occupation in and around Staines in the Bronze Age and on into the early Iron Age (c.1500-600 BC). The locality was favoured with soils that were fertile, easy to work and drained well. The presence of rivers was an additional attraction. The Thames, which in prehistory was a braided river, and the Colne and its many branches provided a focus for rituals. Water gave life to people, crops and animals and it cleansed. More practically it was a means of transport to bring scattered communities together. Many of the chance finds, made before the research and rescue 'digs' of the later 20th century, came from present-day rivers and ancient channels where they had served as propitiatory offerings.

Excavations in the 1970s at Runnymede Bridge (where the A30 and then the M25 cross the Thames) demonstrated this ritual use of the riverbank. The site revealed intense activity including keeping cattle, pigs, sheep and goats and spinning. A hoard of bronzes, sword blades and hilts, some imported and dating from 800 BC, was found placed in pits but there was little other indication of settlement. Nearby, on a site on Petters sports field, which was subsequently bisected by the M25, more bronzes, signs of a bronze smith, hut circles and pits were found but no Iron-Age occupation. Several other sites in Staines, Laleham, Egham, Thorpe Lea and Stanwell have field systems marked by ditches and later by hedges. An urn cremation and burial was found at Stroude Road, Egham and recent trial pits across Manorcrofts fields indicate numerous such Bronze-Age burials. Some, but not all sites had continuity into the Iron Age but there was probably soil exhaustion on many sites.

The coming of the Romans in 54BC probably had no effect on the Staines area. Julius Caesar's main objective was to teach a lesson to Cassivellaunus, whose stronghold was Wheathampstead. Caesar probably crossed the Thames at Brentford, which best fits his account and was on a direct route.

Almost a century elapsed before the invasion of AD43 led by Aulus Plautius.

His first objective was Colchester (Camulodunum), the capital of the Catevellauni. The orthodox interpretation is that the Romans landed in Kent and forded the Thames to set up camp on its northern bank between the Rivers Fleet and Lea. This became London, the focus of trade and main routes and eventually the provincial capital.

One of the routes connected London and Silchester (Calleva) via Brentford and the bridge at Staines. An alternative theory is that the landing was somewhere in the Solent from which the advance would have followed prehistoric tracks to Colchester. It explains the lack of a very early date for London, i.e. before AD50, and the very early date of the Silchester-Colchester route crossing the Thames at Staines.

Whichever explanation is accurate, Staines' key position is important and early in the conquest. It was most likely a posting-station (*mansio*) rather than a changing-station (*mutatio*). The Antonine Itinerary, which was a third-century travellers' guide, omits the smaller changing-stations but includes Staines. There is very little evidence of its ever having been a military site in spite of the discovery of a fine fragment—a cheek piece—from a cavalry helmet dating from AD 60.

The position of the bridge was inferred from that of the medieval bridge. In excavations connected with a second major phase of 'modern' development in the town centre, traces of the Roman bridge at the rear of the town hall were found confirming its closeness to the medieval bridge. The Romans were probably influenced by the soundness of the site and by the existing indigenous crossing. There were most likely well-defined trackways leading to the crossing. The section from the bridge to the foot of Egham Hill (where the line of the Silchester road has been confirmed) was difficult to traverse because of flooding and its constant marshy condition.

The Romans may have been responsible for the original Egham Causeway connecting the bridge to the foot of Egham Hill, much as Thomas de Oxenford was credited with doing centuries later. Other Roman roads converging on the Staines crossing have been postulated: one via the Colne Valley to St Albans (Verulamium) and one from Chichester via Iping to Staines pre-dating Stane Street. These suggestions from E.V. Parrott and D.G. Bird respectively assume the early establishment of Roman Staines.

Until recently the evidence for Roman activity in Staines and Roman exploitation of resources in the surrounding area was sparse. As for the prehistoric period, the finds were mainly from the river or its channels. They included a coin of Trajan found near Savery's Weir in 1858, a group including a bronze sword from a garden in Rosefield Road and, in 1871, evidence of a bath house near the *Angel Inn*. From Wheatsheaf Lane came a fine second-century 'poppy' beaker, and Ernest Ashby, a member of the Staines

banking family, also had a collection of 'found' objects.

The excavation of the Yeoveney Neolithic site in the 1960s revealed extensive agricultural activity in Roman times. Then came a succession of excavations on nine sites in Staines between 1969 and 1973 that produced Roman material from the High Street and Thames Street. The redevelopment of Barclays Bank provided the first major evidence of a Roman settlement in 1970. This included the part of a cavalry helmet already mentioned, the remains of two buildings dating from AD 70 and AD 130-150 together with pottery that included Samian ware and a Spanish amphora. At the Friends Burial Ground there was more pottery, some imported, window and vessel glass, wall plaster, tesserae, hypocaust flues and tiles.

This all indicates quite sophisticated, comfortable living dependent in part on the Thames trade route. Other sites yielded hearths, ovens, wells, a second-century red tessellated floor in situ, stone foundations to buildings and a collyrium stamp of eye ointment implying the presence of a healer.

2 Langham ponds, concealed by the tree line in plate 1, are evidence of the tendency of the Thames to become a braided river in ancient times.

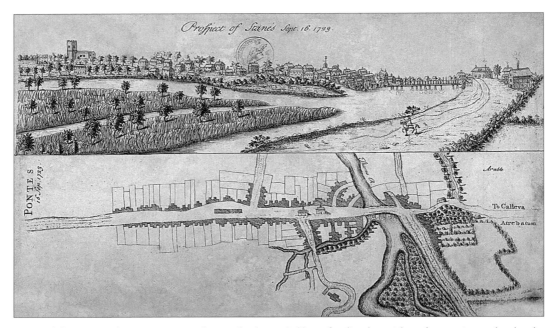

3   Stukeley's view of Staines, 1723. It shows a landscape liable to flooding but with settlement sites – the church and the town – raised up on gravel islands. On the plan, the church is in the bottom foreground, to its right, extensive osier beds and, far right, the Causeway.

Parts of roads and the town's ditches were found in Clarence Street. The latter were perhaps more for the control of flooding than for defence. A very wet site behind the old town tall yielded leather goods including shoes and a double-sided wooden comb all preserved by the wetness. Discoveries in the London Road and Kingston Road suggest that by the fourth century occupation was moving eastwards and away from the wetter west end of the town. On these sites there were cremations and inhumations. North of the High Street, on other gravelly islands, there were signs of enclosed fields. Several sites around Staines indicate the continuity of agriculture into the Roman period and hint at the economic structure that would have provided food and raw materials for the town.

After Rome withdrew its troops from Britain in AD 410 very little light can be shed on Staines, either by archaeology or history, for several centuries. This is a 'dark age' simply because our knowledge is insufficient to throw any light. There is some illumination from the neighbourhood of the lower Thames Valley where archaeological finds at Shepperton and Hanwell from the migration period of the Saxons are considered as associated with early burial sites on the North Downs at Mitcham, Croydon and Orpington. These date from the late sixth century. Place names ending in -ing are present in the Thames Valley, suggesting it was an area of early settlement, while the survival of Celtic names suggests a process of assimilation of the new people into the existing Romano-British landscape.

By the seventh century the migration period was over and the period of history, however sketchy and reliant on folk-memory, begins. As in Roman times, Staines was again on the frontier of political and administrative

4 Floods in 1915 looking across the meadows to the river and the *Anglers' Rest Hotel* (now the *Runnymede Hotel*). The finger post points to Staines Bridge. A finger post at Old Windsor still reads 'Staines, Egham 2½ miles except at high water'.

5 Yeoveney causewayed Neolithic enclosure discovered by aerial survey in 1959, excavated 1961-3 ahead of its destruction by gravel digging and the construction of M25 junction 13. It stood at the tip of the largest gravel island in the Colne valley.

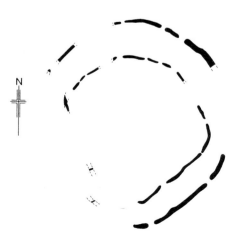

divisions. It would formerly have been part of the territory of St Albans. It became part of the territory of the Middle Saxons (Middlesex), which probably extended more widely than the eventual 11th-century shire, for example to a natural boundary at the foot of the Chilterns.

Middlesex may originally have been one of several territories north and south of the lower Thames. Surrey, literally the 'southern district', was probably another. Middlesex was closely associated with the East Saxons in Essex, where a dynasty of kings was remembered and later incorporated in the Anglo-Saxon Chronicle. By the late seventh century a powerful kingdom in Wessex challenged the advance of Kentish rule and secured control of Surrey, while the East Saxon kingdom seems to have withdrawn from the overlordship of Middlesex. Into this power vacuum there came another dominant kingdom, that of Mercia. All of this placed Staines between Mercian and West Saxon authority, with the Thames becoming the frontier of Wessex. Staines probably regained some of its former importance, but not its

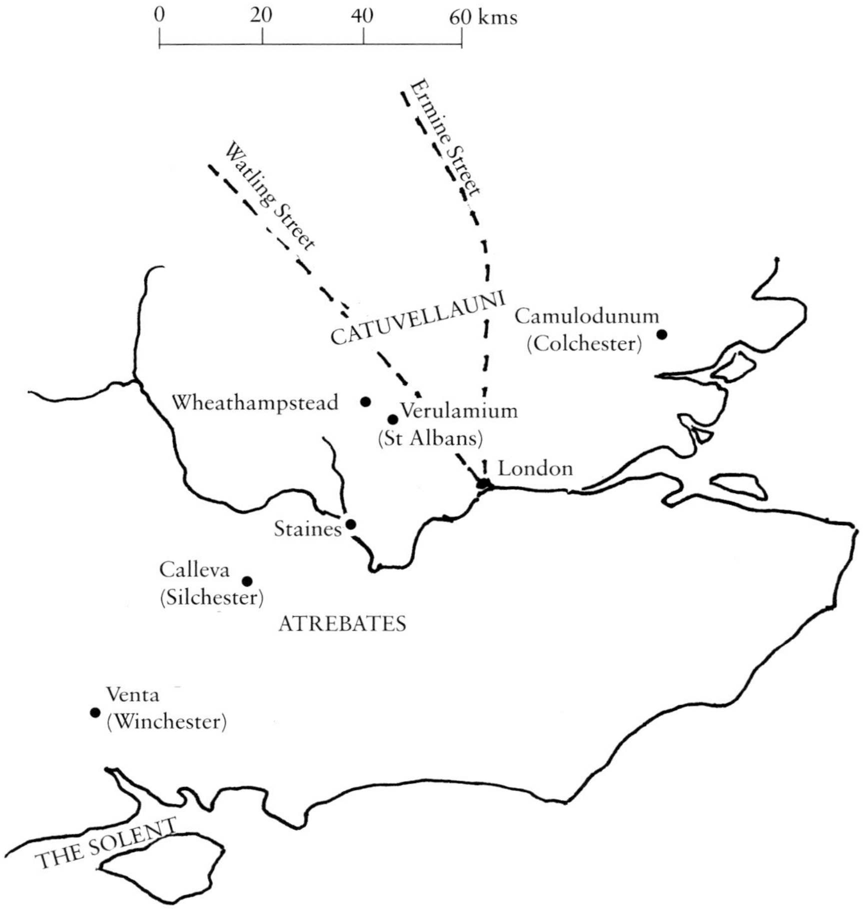

6 Sketch map of South-East Britain showing the strategic position of Staines at the time of the Roman invasions.

size, when the old Roman route from London to Silchester and Winchester, the capital of Wessex, regained its strategic value.

Mercia's advance south and east of its west midland heartland was, in part, to gain access to London and served to help the survival of its trading function. Christianity also revived in the area as a result of the mission to Kent of St Augustine. A bishopric was established in London. These changes helped the revival of London and perhaps ensured that some sort of settlement survived in Staines.

In the 660s, probably in 666, Eorcenwald (Erkenwald), soon to become bishop of London, founded the monastery of Chertsey just four miles south of Staines. The foundation had the support of Egbert, king of Kent and, when it was endowed with more land a few years later, Frithenwold, the only known ruler of Surrey, issued its charter. He was answerable to Wulfhere of Mercia. This is the point at which Egham emerged as part of that gift to the monastery (674).

Both Chertsey and Staines were in the path of the Danish raids that came to

7 The Causeway looking west towards Egham. A Staines landowner, Thomas de Oxenford, was credited with constructing a causeway raised above annual floods from Staines Bridge to Egham Hill in the 13th century. He may have used an existing Roman earthwork.

dominate the ninth century. During King Alfred's campaigns to save Wessex from being conquered by the Danes, he sought to outflank their main base at Reading by advancing along the Colne valley. When peace was made and the land divided between Wessex and the Danelaw, Watling Street marked the frontier, placing Staines firmly within the kingdom of Wessex.

Peace, however, was fragile and the arrangements between the three Danish armies in the Danelaw and Alfred did not affect or check other marauding Danish armies, which roamed over the Low Countries, northern France and south-east England. One sailed up the Thames and wintered in Fulham in 878, the year of the peace. It prompted Alfred to assume overlordship of London. Danish raids from the continent resumed in earnest in 882 and the next year a large army attacked Hampshire and Berkshire. As it withdrew east, it was intercepted, defeated at Farnham by Alfred's eldest son and put to flight. The Danes retreated to Staines in some disorder; many swam the Thames and eventually

took refuge on an island called Thorney between two branches of the River Colne. This army regrouped and for the next three years remained a threat to the Thames Valley while raiding other parts of the country.

After Alfred's death in 899, there was relative peace for almost a century. The kings of Wessex won back the Danelaw and one of them, Edgar (957-975), refounded Chertsey Abbey during the monastic reform movement led by Oswald of Worcester and Aethelwold of Winchester. Priests who had been operating from the abbey over a wide area to minister to many congregations were replaced by celibate monks adhering to a stricter version of the Benedictine rule. There is a tradition that a similar religious house, a minster, also existed in Staines but it is based on no more evidence than a statement of a house for priests 'which is called Staines', in a forged charter of Edward the Confessor. It would seem that the tradition arose from confusion and that the Staines referred to was Stone in Staffordshire. There is, however, a charter of Edgar dated 969 that mentions the Middlesex settlement

8 Sketch map of South-East England, late seventh to early eighth century, showing the frontier situation of Staines between Mercia and Wessex.

by a version of its modern name 'Stana' for the first time. Recent archaeological evidence suggests that in the late Saxon period the focus of settlement moved from the area of the modern market square towards the church, whose foundation has an early Saxon tradition.

Once more Staines experienced the impact of raiders when the Norwegian Olaf Tryggvason embarked on a series of raids around East Anglia and the South Coast. He won a skirmish at Maldon, Essex, in 991, soon after celebrated in one of the great poems of Old English. In 993 he sailed up the Thames unchecked with 93 ships and reached Staines. These attacks continued all the more as the English sought to buy off the raiders. In 1009 a raiding party attacked Chertsey and murdered the abbot and 90 monks. It may have been part of the army that the Anglo-Saxon Chronicle recorded crossing the Thames at Staines to avoid an encounter with the English army. Whether the bridge was still standing or had been replaced by boats is not known.

Chapter Two

THE ABBOT'S MANOR

Staines comes into sharper focus in the 11th century. In 1065, Edward the Confessor was deeply concerned with rebuilding and endowing anew the monastery at Westminster. As part of the endowment he gave the manor of Staines, its church and dependent chapelries (Ashford, Laleham, Teddington and Yeoveney) to this special royal foundation. Staines became one of 60 estates dedicated to providing for and sustaining Westminster Abbey and its 80-odd monks. Most of the estates were in those parts of Middlesex, Essex, Hertfordshire and Surrey nearest to the abbey. The royal grant gave the abbey judicial rights over Staines. These were somewhat poetically expressed in a standard Anglo-Saxon legal phrase as consisting of 'sake and soke, with toll and team and with infangenetheof'. Essentially this meant that the abbot could hold a law court on the estate to deal with the theft of property, in particular of cattle.

Edward's new abbey was consecrated on 28 December 1065. Within a few days, the king was dead and the Bayeux Tapestry depicts his funeral procession approaching the abbey church as a workman is anxiously putting the finishing touches to a weathercock on the tower. In a matter of months, the succession to the throne was claimed and won, with force of arms, by William, Duke of Normandy. Shocking and life-changing as the consequences of the Norman victory at

Hastings were for many, the new ruler did not alter Edward's arrangements. Staines and its dependencies remained part of Westminster's great estates until the abbey itself was dissolved in 1540.

Throughout this period, Staines was administered as a demesne manor. This meant that it was treated as a home farm and its produce, mainly in kind, since it was so near the abbey, was assigned to the maintenance of the abbot's own household. (This very precise assignment dates from 1225, when the abbey's accounting system had become quite sophisticated, but it probably confirms what had for long been the intention.) The household was very grand indeed. The abbot was a powerful, influential figure, often at the heart of the royal court. As well as having political influence, he was the head of a privileged, royal foundation, the custodian of the shrine of a royal saint (the Confessor) and the guardian of the coronation church. His elevated position required a large income in an age when power was normally expressed in wealth and conspicuous consumption. At its zenith in 1100, it has been estimated that the abbey held directly about 60,000 acres.

At the time of King Edward's gift, the value of Staines was reckoned by the inquisitors of Domesday to be £40, which was about one-tenth of the total value of Edward's gifts. Other details from Domesday

The Abbot of St. Peter's holds
In SPELTHORNE Hundred
5 M. STAINES, for 19 hides. Land for 24 ploughs. 11 hides belong to the
lordship; 13 ploughs there. The villagers have 11 ploughs.
   3 villagers, ½ hide each; 4 villagers with 1 hide; 8 villagers
    with ½ virgate each; 36 smallholders with 3 hides; 1 villager
    with 1 virgate; 4 smallholders with 40 acres; 10 smallholders
    with 5 acres each; 5 cottagers with 4 acres each;
    8 smallholders with 1 virgate; 3 cottagers with 9 acres;   **128c**
    12 slaves; 46 burgesses, who pay 40s a year.
   6 mills at 64s; 1 weir at 6s 8d; 1 weir which pays nothing;
    pasture for the village livestock; meadow for 24 ploughs, and
    20s over and above; woodland, 30 pigs; 2 *arpents* of vines.
   4 outliers belong to this manor; they were there before 1066.
  Total value £35; when acquired the same; before 1066 £40.
  This manor lay and lies in the lordship of St. Peter's Church.

9   Entry in Domesday Book describing the manor of Staines.

Book give clues to the kind of place Staines was almost 1,000 years ago.

The most significant fact was the presence of 46 inhabitants described as burgesses or townsmen. In legal terms, this meant they were freemen, tied neither to the manor nor its lord. Their presence did not make Staines a town but it suggests that it had some urban characteristics and should, perhaps, be thought of as a proto-town. The burgesses would have derived their main income from trade and crafts, supplementing it from working small land-holdings. In this Staines was not unique on the abbey's estates, where four other manors also had a sizeable number of burgesses.

The other inhabitants listed in Domesday Book were unfree and derived their income primarily from agriculture. In contrast to the burgesses they were at first liable to regular week-work on the abbot's land, they could not seek to remedy any grievance at the king's courts and they could not have their land without becoming an outlaw, literally placing themselves outside the law. The largest group were 58 bordars (smallholders), most of whom held 10 acres of land. Next on the list were 16 villani (villagers), eight cottars (cottagers) with between three and five acres each and lastly 12 servi (slaves). The smallholders bore the brunt of the work on the home farm assisted by the villagers and cottagers. Their labour was the rent they paid for their own smallholdings. The rate seems to have been three days' labour a week for every five acres. For two-thirds of the population of Staines, sustaining life was a struggle. The abbey's harsh policy of maintaining high rents, whether in labour or cash, ensured that there was little scope for improving output and making profits in a good year. Subsistence farming remained the norm.

Staines was a modest-sized manor with its chief value in its arable land. At the time of Domesday Book it was reckoned that there was sufficient to occupy 24 ploughs, 13 of which were on the abbey's home farm. By the early 14th century the balance had changed, at least in Staines itself. There the abbey had 145 acres of arable while the customary tenants (former smallholders, villagers and cottagers) had 110 and a new class of virtually free tenants (gavelmen) held 65 acres. In the subsidiary manors of Laleham and Yeoveney, the abbey held more than two-thirds of the arable. Over the years there was frequent buying of land by the abbey and some was leased out for long terms. The customary tenants, burgesses and gavelmen were quick to take opportunities to acquire land from waste, of which there was plenty. The process of assarting helped to feed extra mouths and also seems to have

helped the process of loosening the abbey's hold over personal freedom. It may well explain the emergence of gavelmen, exempt from week-work but owing cash rent, by the 14th century.

The manor's arable was set out in huge open fields and a communal system of crop rotation was practised. Usually this involved leaving one field fallow for a year in turn. The acres owned by the abbey and the tenants were scattered across these fields in long, slightly curved strips (to allow a plough to turn) to ensure a reasonable distribution of good and poorer land. Staines produced

10 Staines Church from Lysons' *Beauties of England and Wales*, 1815. The rectorial tithes supported the abbey's guesthouse and infirmary. By 1815, nothing remained of the medieval church but its isolated setting had not altered. It provided space for Stephen Langton's encampment in June 1215.

11 East view of Staines Bridge. The 18th-century view shows the bridge in its medieval position. The river was the main highway for sending the manor's produce by barge over 30 miles downstream to Westminster.

wheat, sometimes sown with a mixture of rye and known as maslin, as well as oats and barley. Wheat and oats provided the staple food for man and beast and were taken from Staines for the direct support of the abbot and his household. Barley was used for brewing beer, which was the everyday drink for monk and ploughman alike. The process of fermenting and heating made it very much safer than water. The river provided the easiest form of transport for these bulky goods directly to the storehouses of the abbey. Wheat, oats, malt and beef long continued to feature in the weekly deliveries from Staines to Westminster.

There were other assets: meadow-land, known locally as meads, and annually enriched by the late winter and spring floods; early pasture for such cattle as could be over-wintered and hay crops to sustain pigs, horses and cattle through the winter.

Cheese, pigs and poultry were products that varied the diet. One of the abbey's records for November 1286 accounts for 53 pigs reared at Laleham and Yeoveney being preserved in the abbey's store at Pyrford (Surrey). The heavily wooded outskirts of the manor provided pannage, grazing land rich in beech-mast and acorns for the pigs. Access to woodland, a share in the meads and in the common pasture, in particular Staines moor, were valuable assets and rights held by all inhabitants. They probably made all the difference to those on the bare margin of subsistence. However, they were not free. The abbey charged extra fines in addition to week-work for customary tenants to use these facilities.

The system changed over very gradually. The abbey was a conservative landlord and held out for decades, even after the Black Death (1348) and its subsequent recurrences had reduced the population by one-third, against responding to change. For most landlords change meant accepting the commuting of labour services for rents, often reduced, since labour had become expensive. The abbey resisted this change and even managed to keep up the level of rents. It tried to prevent free tenants from alienating (selling) their land. Eventually it conceded the right but only under a special licence and on condition that the abbey was given the first refusal of the sale. Such a condition was placed on a certain William, son of Robert de Stanes, when he received the grant of an acre and a messuage (a plot of land with a building). The abbey continued to insist on its right to levy a variety of special fines when, elsewhere, they were fast disappearing. One example from 1395 is Thomas Cook, who had sold his messuage to Robert Lodelowe. Robert had to agree to pay the abbey 1s. 3d. annually or 1s. and three days of reaping.

However, the abbey's tenants became more aware of their economic power and there were occasional signs of assertiveness. In 1490 they had paid a little over £33 in rent but they withheld £1 7s. 9¾d. as a way of adjusting the rent to the general level of the market. In spite of the abbey's conservative administration, the process of change could not be totally resisted. The labour shortage after the Black Death (1351) eventually accelerated the movement to free status and the replacement of customary services by contractual leases. It is hard to believe that Staines would remain immune and ignorant of rumours and news of disturbances nearby. A few miles away, in Harmsworth, there was serious defiance by the servants on the manor that belonged to Holy Trinity, Rouen. The men refused customary duties of doing the lord's haymaking and reaping. They took their complaints about the behaviour of the lord's officials to the manor court and, in 1378, opened sluices to flood the hay rather than reap it. Communication along the Thames would also have ensured that people in Staines were aware of the grievances of

12 The Hythe c.1950, showing 18th-century tile-hung cottages and (left) the *Swan Inn* which was the resort of bargemen and fishermen. At the far end of the *Swan* garden are the remains of the abutment of the first stone bridge, 1798.

13 The Hythe cottages and small bridge which feature from a different angle in figure 14. The Hythe was for many centuries an island and included within the jurisdiction of Staines.

14 The Hythe was the main local landing place for goods carried by river.

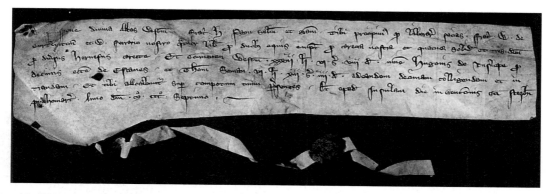

15 Writ sent to the bailiff of Staines, Hugh of Ruislip, by Abbot Walter de Wenlok (1283-1307). The abbot commands the bailiff to send the tithes of Staines Church (£33 6s. 8d.) to the convent at Westminster.

the Peasants' Revolt in 1381. No disturbances were recorded in Staines. Perhaps the process of gaining free or virtually free status and of commuting services to money rents had developed sufficiently to avoid unrest.

Because of its proximity to London, Staines was affected by the development of a prosperous class of royal officials and city dignitaries such as aldermen and senior liverymen. Such men might anachronistically be called a rising middle class. They were keen to acquire land and their interest and wealth encouraged the growth of a market in land. In 1337 Roger Belet, butler to Edward III's queen, Philippa of Hainault, was granted the manor of La Hyde in Laleham and subsequently purchased other land in Staines. His name is preserved locally as 'the Billetts'. Belet was a lawyer and had already acquired an estate in Reading. In 1366 he sold his Laleham estate to the abbey but provided a life interest for his wife, Agnes, until her death in 1382.

As well as owning the manor of Staines, Westminster Abbey owned the church and its glebe land together with four chapelries—Ashford, Laleham, Teddington and Yeoveney. It was a valuable property given a worth of £46 13s. 14d. in 1291. The church's main endowment was 55 acres of glebe. Domesday

Book's entry for Buckinghamshire records a rent of 6s. 8d. owing to the church of Staines from land in East Burnham. It is likely that there was a church on the present site by 1100. Lysons writes of Saxon work but he probably meant Norman. The first mention of the church in the Westminster Abbey records is 1179 and there are other references in papal bills during the 12th century confirming the abbey's ownership. There was further papal confirmation in 1217-8 in a decision that also mentioned a vicarage. This is an example of papal concern at the large number of gifts of churches to religious houses in the previous century. The appointment of vicars (literally deputies) was a policy devised to ensure that the parishioners were provided with spiritual care. In Staines, as in other such parishes, the church's income, primarily from tithes, was divided: the so-called great tithe (the tax of a tenth on cereal crops) was apportioned to the abbey as rector, while the small tithe and altar offerings sustained the vicar. When the abbey apportioned income more exactly to different departments and functions of its work, the rectory of Staines supported the abbey guesthouse and infirmary. In 1381 the church had a clerk, William, who assisted the vicar, Thomas Gilmyn. Both appear in the clerical poll tax returns for the archdeaconry

16 Two more writs from the abbot: the first ordering a payment of 3s. 6d. for work done by a forester; and the second requesting supplies of wheat, oats and calves to be sent speedily (next Saturday) to Westminster.

of Middlesex. Laleham was also listed with a vicar named William but there was no mention of the other chapelries for which Staines was supposed to be responsible.

Staines' importance as a river crossing, carrying the road from London to Winchester, was confirmed by repeated royal grants of pontage, tolls for using the bridge. The aim was to ensure that the bridge wardens

17 King John and King Philip Augustus of France exchange the kiss of peace after the sealing of Magna Carta.

kept the bridge in repair. Until 1410, it was probably the only one west of London. This strategic position no doubt gave impetus to the development of features of a town: a sizeable population of free men, trade and manufacture. Confirmation of the trend came in 1218, with the grant of a market to be held weekly on Sundays. A little later the day was changed to Friday. The modern arrangement of the bridge and market square obscures the natural connection made in 1218 when the bridge was sited downstream and ran straight into the market area. Another recognition of Staines' importance as a hub of economic activity was the grant of a fair, in 1228, to be held annually on the four days following the feast of the Ascension.

Royal records contain a number of references to the bridge and, in particular, to its maintenance. Twice, in 1222 and 1261, timber was brought from Windsor forest for its repair. During the same century there were several renewals of the grant of pontage and in 1376 charging tolls on traffic passing under the bridge raised additional funds. Across the river, on the Surrey side, was the Hythe, a former island, a point of loading and unloading goods. Its importance as a landing stage by the bridge was reinforced

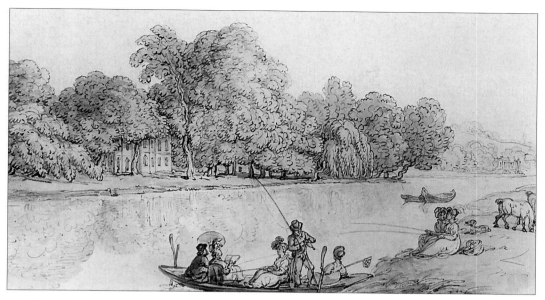

18 Elegant fishing party on Magna Carta Island (Thomas Rowlandson). The nunnery of Ankerwyke and its land in Wraysbury and Egham came into the hands of Sir Philip Harcourt in the 18th century. His family promoted the (mistaken) notion that Magna Carta was secured on their island.

by the inclusion of some of its tenements within the jurisdiction of Staines. Another feature of the Surrey side was the causeway, a raised roadway as much as six feet above ground level, connecting the bridge to the foot of Egham Hill. It allowed traffic to pass along the London to Winchester highway even during the winter and also acted as a flood barrier. The alternative route was a lengthy detour via Chertsey and the higher ground to the south-west, eventually, after crossing the River Bourne, rejoining the highway near Virginia Water lake.

The origins of the causeway came to light a hundred years later during an inquiry at Guildford to discover who was responsible for its maintenance and repair. The benefactor was Thomas de Oxenford, a wool merchant whose trade depended on sound communications. It seems he was also a substantial landowner in Staines. The year of the inquiry was inauspicious: 1350 marked the height of the Black Death, which, for a while, paralysed economic life. The

unresolved matter was raised again in 1368. Then, and on several subsequent occasions, the abbot of Chertsey, as lord of the manor of Egham, escaped responsibility. Richard II attempted a solution by appointing two men, possibly the existing wardens of the bridge, to collect a local tax to repair both the bridge and the causeway. Fifty years later the matter was still being disputed. The folk of Egham refused pontage because firstly they thought the abbot should do the job and secondly because they believed that all the money collected was used on the bridge, to the neglect of the causeway. It was a short-sighted quarrel that damaged both communities. The issue remained unresolved for another century.

In the early summer of 1215, Staines was at the centre of a national crisis. A group of northern lords had raised a rebellion against King John, objecting to his demand for their military service in a forlorn campaign to try to regain Normandy (which John had lost in 1204). The diplomatic skill of Stephen

19 King John and Magna Carta from a painting by Benjamin West, a Quaker and friend of the Ashby family of Staines.

Langton, Archbishop of Cantebury, staved off outright civil war but he needed time to fine-tune an agreement based on Henry I's coronation charter. The royal party was at Windsor. Staines provided just the place to settle the rebels during the final days of negotiation. Langton and the barons were granted a safe conduct during May and encamped round the church. There Langton consecrated two Welsh bishops. The two groups converged halfway at Runnymede for the sealing of the draft articles and the issuing of Magna Carta under the Great Seal four days later.

Whether locals were sorry or relieved when the court and barons dispersed is impossible to know. The craftsmen probably enjoyed more trade but the encampments would have ruined much of the first crop of hay on the meads. At the time the significance of the great charter was obscure. However, a forest charter of 1217 was a direct consequence. It relaxed many of the most irksome restrictions on folk living on or near land designated as forest. Ten years later a specific benefit to Staines was the royal charter taking Staines and its warren out of forest law 'so all men may cultivate their land and assart the woods therein'. At the same time nuns of the order of St John of Jerusalem living within the warren of Staines were allowed to give free rein to their dogs to protect both their persons and their sheepfolds.

Chapter Three

Medieval Egham

Like its neighbour Staines, Egham was also a monastic manor. It had been part of the endowment of Chertsey Abbey since the mid-10th century when King Edgar replaced priests with monks. The abbey's early history was punctuated by episodes of violence and destruction both before and after the Conquest. This explains some of the loss in value of its nearest manors, Chertsey, Chobham, Egham and Thorpe. Egham was the abbey's second most valuable manor. However, by comparison with Westminster Abbey, Chertsey's wealth and importance was modest, although its abbots were mitred and retained good relations with the Crown to the abbey's benefit. One of its valuable privileges was having hunting rights in Windsor forest and the right to exclude the king's officers from its demesne manors. As with Staines, there was also the privilege of the abbot holding his own court in each manor.

The abbey's foundation charter describes the boundaries of Egham. These were so important that each generation learned them, usually by the practice of annually 'beating the bounds'. It mattered little that pointers, such as the old apple tree, the three trees and the maple, soon vanished; the folk memory was sound enough to preserve the knowledge. A 17th-century notebook found at Rusham and used mainly for recording court cases in Windsor also contained a copy of the ancient boundary translated into contemporary English.

The abbey's possessions were composed of its spiritualities, amounting to about one-fifth of the whole in value, and temporalities. The former consisted of the tithes from churches on its manors where the abbey was the impropriator and pensions paid by churches where it was not. The temporalities were the manors that yielded rents, goods and services.

Within Egham there was freehold land, which reduced some services but whose holders had a good deal of autonomy and accumulated land. There was ample opportunity to incorporate land from waste, the process called assartment. From these holdings subordinate manors came into being. In Egham these have been identified as Imworth, Milton, Rusham, Trotesworth, Portnall and Ankerwyke. The rest of the land was bond or villein land. Those who worked it were liable to labour services and cultivating the abbot's land while trying to look after their own holdings in what remained of each week. They were subject to a range of taxes: the heriot (the best beast) on inheriting the property, the merchet on a daughter's marriage and tallage, an arbitrary tax. The conditions of service were, therefore, much the same as those experienced in Staines.

Although Chertsey's records are patchy, many being lost in the fire that destroyed the

In GODLEY Hundred
21 The Abbey holds EGHAM itself. Before 1066 it answered for 40
    hides, now for 15 hides. Land for 40 ploughs. In lordship 2 ploughs;
    25 villagers and 32 smallholders with 10 ploughs.
    Meadow, 120 acres; woodland, 50 pigs from pasturage;
    from grazing, 25 pigs.
    Value before 1066 £40; now £30 10s.
    Jocelyn holds 3 hides of this land which were in the Abbey's
    lordship before 1066.

20   Domesday Book's description of Egham.

abbey in 1235 and the riots in 1381, what survives is of particular value for Egham. In 1307, a monk from the Egham family of Rutherwyk was elected abbot. John Rutherwyk proved an able and vigorous administrator. The cartulary recording the abbot's 'acta', his legal decisions, and containing confirmation of earlier decisions, survives with some later, 15th-century additions. It also contains a fragment of a survey of all the abbey's estates, which refers to Egham. With the manorial court record, a vivid and often detailed source of material, it is possible to build a picture of life in the half-century before the Black Death. It was the high noon of manorial farming.

In the years before Rutherwyk's election, the abbey had followed a policy of taking back land formerly leased out. Rutherwyk continued this programme. One method was by encouraging pious folk to surrender their land in old age to the abbey. In return the abbey provided a pension, mainly in kind, for life. Not only did this 'corrody' offer a secure old age but it also secured the monks' prayers for the donors. Rutherwyk also followed the practice of either purchasing or exchanging many small plots of land that filled gaps in the abbey's holdings.

One example, in 1316, was the purchase of two small plots, together amounting to a mere two acres, which joined up two of the abbey's plots. In 1320 Rutherwyk tidied up a part of the abbey's lands at Loderlake, which was on the western boundary of Egham where three shires, Berkshire, Buckinghamshire and Surrey, meet. The nunnery of Ankerwyke, across the river in Wraysbury, had acquired several plots in this area and was persuaded to exchange them for lands of the abbey at Purnesh on the slopes of Cooper's hill.

The Loderlake lands had been acquired for the abbey indirectly. It may have been done secretly to avoid rousing opposition to the abbot's keen acquisition of land. Walter de Clerkenwell, a chaplain later found a living by the abbey, accumulated land amounting to more than 100 acres using money provided by Rutherwyk and having the professional aid of the abbot's attorneys, John Gold and William de Stanes, to carry out the conveyances. Previous owners or their descendants were sought out to put their names to quit claims that they had truly surrendered their rights of ownership. Walter then made over the whole estate to the abbey, receiving it back for his use during his lifetime at a nominal rent. He was also to be rewarded with the commemoration in prayers of the anniversary of his death.

The scheme almost failed when it was challenged in the king's court at Southwark. Some of the transactions were claimed to be illegal by three plaintiffs: Thomas, the young heir to the Middleton lands–the manor of Milton–Audomer at the Hamme, a freeholder in Ingfield (Engelfield Green) and Sir John Gacelyn, holder of the abbey's knight's fee, which meant he performed military service on the abbot's behalf. The case went in the abbot's favour, the plaintiffs were fined £20 but the abbot remitted two-thirds of the fine 'and forever quietly pardoned' the three. Rutherwyk's next major acquisition was the estate of Walter de Gloucester, a leading courtier. Walter's widow, Hawisa, was persuaded to sell to the abbey 200 acres of arable, 20 of pasture, five messuages and five tofts. Its rent yield was £4 13s. 4d. a

year. The estate, spread through Chertsey, Egham and Thorpe, was land that the abbey had formerly owned and then alienated. Rutherwyk's actions were a response to the state of the market. Land was becoming more valuable as a growing population increased demand and therefore raised the value of rents and services.

The manorial court records provide glimpses of the demands laid by usage and tradition on the abbot's tenants. Free or unfree, they all had obligations determined by custom. The bulk of the Egham manor consisted of 'bond' or unfree land and carried the heaviest burden of services in money, kind and labour. When a man inherited a piece of

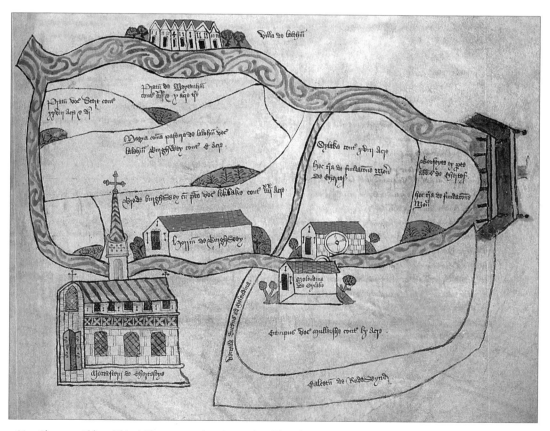

21 Chertsey Abbey. This 15th-century plan shows the abbey demesne encircled by the Thames and a millstream. The abbey church is in the left foreground, the great barn to its right and far right are two mills powered by the stream. On the right is Chertsey Bridge, built in 1410, just before this map was drawn.

22   Chertsey tile from a pavement decorated with stylised foliage.

land he was formally admitted in court before the abbot's steward, or his representative and a jury of fellow tenants. Freeholders paid a fine, unfree a heriot, their best beast. The records for Egham contain the example of a bull valued at 8s., a horse worth 6s. 8d. and, from a much poorer tenement, a sheep worth 10d.

When the heir was a child – in 1320, John de Denham was nine years old – his mother made the claim in the manorial court and paid a heriot and a fine of 5s. for wardship. The child came of age at 16 when the wardship ceased. He would then be admitted to his land, usually with the proviso that he had to reserve a portion for his mother. On several occasions, tenants came to court to testify that they had no animals, sometimes no goods, with which to pay a heriot. If the jury accepted this as the truth, they were admitted.

Land holdings were quite small, usually consisting of a messuage, a plot of land with a house, and a half-virgate. As in Staines, the virgate in Egham was calculated as 30 acres. Again like Staines, the land holding was unlikely to be totally enclosed, but was

scattered throughout the large open fields around Egham, and had an allowance of meadow on the Thameside meads. Some holdings had rough pasture often illegally enclosed from waste or common land. These were called purprestures and gained acceptance when a fine was paid. The neighbouring royal park and the long periods when Egham itself had been brought under forest jurisdiction provided opportunities for poaching, collecting wood, which was precious for building and burning, and grazing beasts. The latter was a limited right (of agistment) paid for by the requirement of providing hay from the manor to feed the Windsor deer through the winter. It was a custom that continued until the end of the 17th century. The poorest tenants had no more than a cottage with its curtilage.

Some tenants accumulated tenements that, by the standards of the time, were small estates. Adam in the Hale had a messuage and a virgate of serf land, five acres of freehold land, one and a half acres of Levedycroft, which was prone to flooding and where he had a duty to maintain the drains, and half a tenement bought from William le Whyte. Adam was a prosperous villager but that did not bar him from acquiring freehold land. The manorial court could be flexible in allowing the purchase of land and in allowing parts of a man's holding to be surrendered to meet the needs of his family. Walter de Bakeham was given leave to surrender a cottage and curtilage at Prewelle (the modern Prune Hill) to provide for an adult son and daughter. He paid a fine of 6d. for that transaction. Land could also be exchanged, often for the same reason as the abbot's exchanges, to consolidate a holding, running together two or three strips in the open fields. Thomas de Langham and his wife, who appear to be relatively prosperous, owning two and possibly three cottages, were allowed to exchange half a virgate with Robert and Mary Hale. The Hales were allowed the right of reversion and both couples were to have half a cottage at Eghamhelde (Egham Hill).

Sometimes jurors were required to determine the ownership of land and its status, whether free or bond. Such details were not documented and therefore local

23 Chertsey tile from a pavement showing the zodiac.

knowledge going back over the generations was relied on. The collective memory was helped by the custom of describing a piece of land by its position and the neighbouring lands abutting. The names of owners of abutting lands were often not the current ones and so the lands acquired a history. In 1344 a dispute over the ownership of an acre of land arose between William atte Ashe and his wife Mathilda and the occupier of the acre, Alice in the Hale and her son John, who was a minor. The jury found in favour of William, for it said Mathilda had inherited the land. Several cases of a similar kind arose because a woman's inheritance had caused confusion. One reason for this was the practice of a man changing his name to his wife's where she was the inheritor of land. The man often used an alias that continued over several generations.

The Imworth name would have died out on Robert's death since he had only two daughters to succeed to his freehold lands. One daughter married Simon de Rutherwyk, possibly the abbot's father or his elder brother, and the other, elder daughter married Robert Burton. He was first mentioned in 1296-7 being granted a tenement in Egham by Bartholomew of Winchester, Rutherwyk's predecessor. On her marriage, the eldest daughter, Sara, received her father's estate in which he kept a lifetime's interest. Burton took the Imworth name and built up a substantial tenement on the south-eastern side of Egham. It came to be regarded as a subordinate manor with land south of the Staines-Windsor highway as far as the Glanty, a wood called Barnswick, probably on Egham Hill, land on Prune Hill and south of Egham field where Great Fosters was later built. The capital messuage or manor house was near the vicarage.

Matters more disturbing to the peace of the manor than settling property rights in court were the outbreaks of crime and violence described in the manorial records as 'enormia'. One occasion was an attack on one of the abbot's servants, Thomas le Wodeward and his servant by Thomas de Miltone and John atte Lampulle. They assaulted and injured Thomas Wodeward and his man using swords, bows and arrows, stole a horse and caused £40 worth of damage. The defendants pleaded not guilty and a jury was called for a trial at Michaelmas. Infuriatingly, the folio is torn at this point.

The abbot's rule was efficient and vigorous but he was not beyond taking the law into his own hands. Bartholomew had a new, turbulent and quarrelsome family called de Wallingford in Thorpe. One of their many disputes was with an Egham freeholder, Thomas de Suddington. (Luddington may be a corruption of his name.) The Wallingfords drove him from some of his property. Bartholomew, impatient with 'due process', led a raid of 80 men, including Egham freeholders such as Henry de Middleton, Simon de Rutherwyk,

24 Ruins of Chertsey Abbey, 1850. Nowadays nothing remains above ground because at the dissolution the royal mason, John Nedeham, supervised the careful demolition. The stone was taken to Hampton Court.

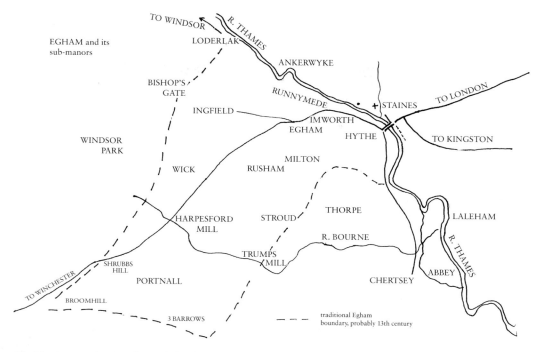

25 Sketch map showing the probable line of the boundary of Egham based on a traditional list of landmarks which may be Saxon in origin but, more likely, date from the 13th century.

Robert atte Strode, Thomas and Adam de Suddington and Robert de Imworth. In their attack on the Wallingford property, trees were felled and possessions carried off. The abbot was fined 100 shillings in the king's court but after having softened up his opposition he managed, through the law, to drive away the Wallingfords, apart from one tenement in Egham.

There were no heirs to the Rutherwyk lands in Egham. After Simon's death there remained William and his wife, childless, and a sister, Avice, unmarried. They solved not only their pension needs but also provided handsomely for the good of their souls by formally surrendering their lands and all their possessions to the abbey. They received, in return, a lifetime leaseback of their lands and an allowance in kind, a corrody, of food and clothing, which was spelled out in detail in their agreement. Daily they received four

loaves, a gallon of conventual ale and two dishes from the convent kitchen. In addition they each had a new outfit of clothing, minutely described since the quality of cloth and type of fur trimming signalled one's social standing. The clothes were presented at Christmas. They were also annually entitled to a quantity of cheese, two cartloads of hay, one bullock, three fattened pigs and, at Martinmas (11 November), 16 pounds of candles to see them through the darkest times of winter. The whole estate was larger than that acquired through Walter de Clerkenwell: 120 acres of arable, 10 acres of meadow, 12 of pasture, 20 of wood, 12 of heath, three messuages, three alder patches and 12s. 5d. in rent. Having her messuage at la Strode guaranteed for life protected Avice, the sister.

Rutherwyk looked after the fabric of his manor, rebuilding the church, repairing a

26 St John the Baptist's Church, Egham. This 1804 watercolour shows the church very much as it was rebuilt by Abbot John Rutherwyk in the early 14th century. On the left is a corner of the manor farm granary raised on steddle stones to deter vermin.

dovecote and keeping the causeway to Staines bridge in repair. He acquired Harpesford mill from the king. The other mill in the manor was Trumps mill, only half of which belonged to the abbot. All these were sound investments. Another was allowing the hermit, William de Karewent, to build a house at the Hythe by the bridge for 1d. rent. William would doubtless have encouraged pious travellers to give generously and, equally doubtless, the abbot would have ensured he had a percentage of the income.

Rutherwyk's abbacy (1307-46) coincided with a period of great population growth and pressure on land. Few holdings remained vacant even if no heirs could be found. The need for more land to be made available led to illegal enclosures from wasteland (purprestures) and utilisation of headlands and margins in the open fields. Rutherwyk exploited this situation to the abbey's advantage. His good management is represented by a survey of his lands that he began in 1316 but of which only a fragment survives. Fortunately this includes Egham. The manor was the abbey's second most valuable possession. It had 194½ acres of arable in demesne valued at £6 12s. 9¼ d. in rents. The lands were distributed in the open fields: Egham Field south of the main street, Hythe Field following the line of the river to the east and then southwards towards Thorpe and Chertsey, and Hamworth Field probably indicated by the modern Hummer road and stretching north of the main street towards the meads. It was linked to two other smaller open fields nearby: Rude Field (12½ acres) and Yard Mead (10½ acres). Together with some even smaller pieces of arable in the same area, this arrangement suggests that extra common arable had been taken into cultivation from pasture and even meadow near to the river. In subsequent centuries Yard Mead featured solely as meadowland adjoining Runnymede.

In addition to arable, the abbot held about 55 acres of meadow, of which 11 were on Runnymede. Other possessions listed are the capital messuage near the church with cottages much in need of repair, Harpesford mill, the quay at Woodhaw, tolls on the river, fishing rights and the right to cut withies and take herbage from heath land. Taxes included a charge on every brewhouse, a tax on pigs put out into the woods for acorns (pannage), fines, heriots, reliefs and court fees. Services and crops due from each sown acre were carefully calculated as well as the duties of ploughing, harrowing, sowing and cutting expected collectively from the tenants.

The monetary value of the manor's income, probably for 1343, is contained in part of the steward's accounts. It came to a little over £90, of which almost £20 derived from the best quality wheat. Rents yielded almost £18 whilst the meat, eggs and cheese produced for the abbey were calculated according to standard prices applied throughout the abbey's manors.

By the 15th century a significant change had come over the manor. There was no longer population pressure on the land. The

27   Egham High Street from an 1830 pencil and watercolour by Edward Hassell (1811-52). Egham was a 'street' village with outlying settlements: Egham Wick, the Hythe, Imworth, Milton, Rusham, Stroude and Trotesworth.

28 Milton Place in 1865 as rebuilt by Edgell Wyatt Edgell. He purchased the whole of Milton manor which, in 1519, became part of the endowment of Corpus Christi College, Oxford. For the previous 400 years it had belonged to the Middleton family.

effects of the Black Death and subsequent outbreaks of plague and epidemics gradually prevented the population from recovering from the huge losses in 1350. Labour became scarcer and it became difficult to find tenants for vacant land. Plots that were uncultivated for a few years quickly lost value and as a result their rents were reduced. There ensued a domino effect on other rents. Services in kind were replaced by monetary commutation. Most eloquent comments on the changes are statements in the abbey cartulary. John of Thorp was discharged of 10s. 2d. from his rent of 52s. 2½d.; instead of 2s. 1d. for a messuage at Halsham, John de Milton was asked for 16d. and, at the Hythe, a plot called Attcroft had its rent halved. There was a serious outbreak of plague in 1434; it was followed a year later by more rent reductions. A telling comment in 1435 was the following: 'for cause of pestilence happening more than usual whereby the people and tenants in the like vills are daily decreasing [lands] lie uncultivated and derelict and the aforesaid particles of land are now of less value'.

In 1440 a similar story emerged from statements of land lying derelict, and rent reductions of up to 50 per cent were granted. There was 'rarity of servers, scarcity of cultivators and the pestilence of the peoples more than usually happening whereby people and tenants are daily departing'. There appears to have been less resistance at Chertsey to accepting the decay of villeinage than at Westminster Abbey. The process, however, had an inevitable force; resistance merely delayed the outcome. Villagers transmuted into copyholders and soon were hardly distinguishable, in economic status, from freeholders.

Chapter Four

THE REFORMATION

The Reformation tends popularly to be understood as a great act of state originating in Henry VIII's need for a legitimate heir and the consequent quarrel with the pope. This obscures the huge and revolutionary impact it had on the lives of ordinary people. Within a generation, those familiar features of daily life, in Staines and across the land, which brought solace for the present and hope for the future beyond the grave, were first challenged and then largely removed. With the wanton destruction that characterised Edward VI's reign, many people's comforting glimpses of heaven were also destroyed. Colourful images, carved crosses, processional banners, the great statues of the rood screen, stained glass and precious service books, many illuminated by hand, were smashed by royal commissioners and the church interiors white-washed. In some ways the mid-1500s must have resembled the Maoist concept of continuing revolution as the political and religious pendulum swung back and forth between Catholic and Protestant.

In Staines and Egham there was the additional change of landlords. The personal and economic relationships that had been in place for five to six centuries between the Abbeys of Westminster and Chertsey and their Thameside manors were broken. The familiar representatives of the abbeys were replaced by new, sometimes rapidly changing landlords, eager for a profitable investment or a quick sale.

Not only did the appearances of the churches change but so also did their role. Hitherto St Mary's in Staines and St John the Baptist in Egham had been the most substantial, important and dominant building in each parish. What was taught in the church, more by symbols and ceremonies than by words, provided an unchallenged framework of belief, hierarchy and morality. It pervaded every corner of daily living: education, ethics, entertainment as well as the social fabric of village life derived from the church. The church's calendar was the one that everyone used. It provided the holidays, literally the saints' days that mercifully punctuated the unremitting labour of earning a living.

Before Protestantism was unleashed as a challenge to the pope's authority, there were scarcely any indications of religious dissent in the locality. However, in the Chilterns there survived some small communities of Lollards. These were adherents to a movement associated with John Wycliff. He had argued that scripture, rather than the Church and pope, was the chief authority for Christ's teaching. Lollards thus foreshadowed Protestantism and were the first to produce English versions of the Bible so that it was accessible to all who could read.

There was a Lollard priest in the neighbouring village of Horton, one Robert

29 St Mary's Church, Staines. This 18th-century engraving shows the extended chancel and the tower, rebuilt in 1631. The churchwarden's accounts for the 17th century suggest that repairs were badly needed. Melting down the lead from the north aisle, in 1643, for the parliamentary cause contributed to the decay.

Freeman, and at least one Lollard family in Staines who read the English Bible, but in such secrecy that the servants were first sent out. This may well have been the Durdant household at Yeoveney. The Durdants had a long-established Lollard connection. The will of Nicolas in 1538 had none of the formulaic phrases seeking the aid of the Virgin and saints to help the soul's journey. Instead Nicholas trusted 'undoubtedly that by the merits of His only son Jesus Christ to be one of the elect'. Richard Atwick of Egham, who also had property in Laleham, may have been a Lollard sympathiser. His will is unusual for the time (1516) in making no pious bequests.

Other local wills that survive from the 15th and early 16th centuries demonstrate the devotion of parishioners to the parish church. They illustrate the conviction that the saints, headed by the Virgin Mary, could be enlisted to help them in the trials of life and in purgatory.

The earliest of the Egham wills is that of Richard Middleton (died 1415), a member of the family that held the manor of Milton. He left four sheep, which would have been added to local flocks and treated as part of the church's 'store'. Income from the sale of their fleece or lambs was to maintain the light on St Mary's altar. He also left 12d. for the light before the crucifix and half a mark (6s. 8d.) for the church fabric.

In 1424 John Hanhampstede, a citizen of London, left the residue of his estate, after making provision for his family, for

30 Horton Church where the Milton family worshipped, and in the early 16th century the parson was inclined to the Lollard cause. It was the neighbouring parish to Yeoveney where the Durdant family presaged the advent of Protestantism by reading the Bible in English.

pious purposes. He gave £20 for the church fabric, the repair of the belfry, a priest to celebrate masses for him for a year and for the lights before the altars of the Holy Cross and St Mary. William Clerk, in 1490, left 4d. for each of the lights on these same altars, Robert Ode (1464) left 12d. for wax tapers for the 'rodeloft' and a further 12d. for the light of St Mary.

These bequests serve to underline the importance of the images, altars and candles belonging to the parish's special saints. In a world illuminated only by expensive wax candles or cheaper and smelly rush lights, the church was an oasis of light, colour and movement. It gave reassurance in a harsh, uncertain world. In both parishes, there was special devotion to the Holy Cross and St Mary. There was a fraternity in each church dedicated to the Holy Cross.

The Staines fraternity owed its foundation, in 1456, to John Lord Berners, Sir John Wenlock and a group of parishioners. It had a constitution that provided for two wardens and a number of brethren and sisters. It attracted modest endowments and gifts in kind and cash, as the wills illustrate. It had an annual income of £11 17s. 6d. in 1548 and provided the rent for its own priest's accommodation. It made gifts to the poor and spent 6s. 8d. on a yearly sermon. When it was dissolved, in Edward's reign, an inventory of its goods and plate would have been made, but sadly it was lost.

The fraternity's chaplain, Sir William Gale, who died in 1518, typically left a number of bequests to the Church. (He was not a knight: 'sir' was a respectful title for a priest.) The main ones were 3s. 4d. to St Paul's in London; 3s. 4d. to the Rood (Holy Cross) chapel in the church of Staines; 3s. 4d. for the high altar light and 4d. for 'our Lady light'. In neighbouring Littleton, there was also a chantry chapel and chaplain. Its

31 Sir William Dolben as Recorder of London. He was also brother to the Dean of Westminster who granted him the lease of the manor of Yeoveney following the demise of the Durdant's lease.

dedication was to St Mary Magdalene. Its chaplain, in addition to gifts similar to those left to Staines, left 10s. to the friars minor to say prayers for his soul and those of his parents, brothers and sisters.

The changes that the king's 'great matter' brought about were slow to affect parish churches, unless there were active Protestants in the area. There is no evidence of any in Staines. However, news from London travelled quickly. Rumours and gossip about the king's divorce, the marriage to Anne Boleyn and her unpopularity with the Londoners who greeted her coronation progress with silence would all have reached the Staines area. The constant movement of people and goods along the river would have ensured this. In 1535 there would probably have been shock at the barbaric treatment of the monks of Syon and John Hale, the vicar of Isleworth, for their refusal to acknowledge the new line of succession to the throne.

32 Prince Henry in the hunting field, *c*.1605. James I granted the prince the manor of Egham, which passed to his brother Charles in 1612.

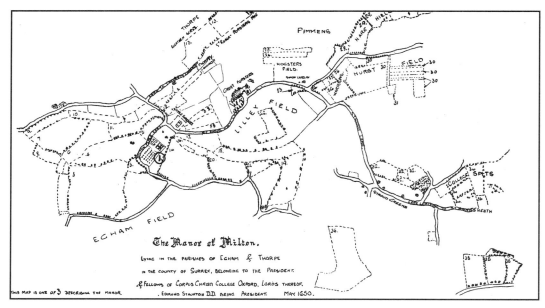

33   Plan of the fields and strips scattered in Egham and Thorpe which comprised the manor of Milton. Milton Place is at (1).

Some changes were probably accepted. The quarrel with the pope was nothing new, although on this occasion it was extreme. Nevertheless, the order to remove his name from the service books was generally accepted. Certainly people would have sensed that a huge change was underway when, eventually, the Bible in English was placed in the church. Although ordered in 1538 it is unlikely that one appeared in Staines until at least 1541.

Of more immediate concern were the consequences of the injunctions issued in 1536. These attacked the idolatrous use of images, rejected relics and discouraged pilgrimages. Priests were ordered to preach against them. They also removed a number of saints' days from the calendar. Among these was the September feast of the Holy Cross. This would not have been welcomed in Staines. No-one likes losing a holiday.

All these changes were soon overtaken by the decision to close down the smaller monasteries, a process that began in 1536

and which included Chertsey Abbey. The process was brutal, destructive and based on fabricated reports of widespread indolence and immorality. There were rebellions in Lincolnshire and Yorkshire (the Pilgrimage of Grace). But in Chertsey there was no resistance. Abbot Cordrey was realistic in recognising he could not outwit the ruthless methods of Thomas Cromwell's officers.

With characteristic disregard for objectivity, most of the monks were charged with gross immorality and the whole house described as 'the foulest set of monks in the kingdom'. The deed of surrender was signed on 6 July 1537. The abbot had already prudently sold many possessions and granted extraordinary long leases on land. For a time it seemed as though there would be a reprieve of a kind. The community was transferred to Bisham, itself recently dissolved, but then re-endowed with property from nearby abbeys. Then it was dissolved again.

The king had, from the outset of this policy, wanted to gain possession of three of the abbey's manors, Chertsey, Egham and Thorpe, and thus extend his Windsor hunting grounds. Once he had suppressed Westminster Abbey, in January 1540, he was able to extend them further east by adding the manor of Staines. Westminster was a great prize, its wealth being second only to Glastonbury's. Within months, the scramble to acquire its former manors was underway. The new owners bought a stake in the Henrician reformation.

In Staines, one family, the Durdants, remained secure, surviving these upheavals. They continued as lessees of one of Westminster Abbey's manors at Yeoveney. Since 1366, Yeoveney had ceased to be farmed directly by the abbey and was leased to Thomas Durdant, a janitor of the abbey and a freeholder in Denham, Buckinghamshire. When Elizabeth refounded Westminster Abbey with a dean and 12 prebendaries, Thomas's descendant, Andrew, acquired the lease on a term of three lives. Another Andrew, either his son or grandson, was a prominent member of the Staines community in the early 17th century, serving as churchwarden and chief constable. Eventually, this Andrew's son (or grandson) Charles was deprived of the lease in 1665. The new lease was then granted to William Dolben, the dean's brother and a justice of the King's Bench. The manor house at Yeoveney was probably the building that survived as Yeoveney Farm.

Westminster Abbey's former main manor of Staines remained in the Crown's possession until 1613, when King James I granted it to a courtier, Thomas Lord Knyvett. He was a career courtier from a gentry family in Norfolk. His grandfather, another Thomas (of Buckenham), had been Master of the Horse to Henry VIII. The younger Knyvett was keeper of Whitehall Palace and a gentleman of the bedchamber

to both Elizabeth and James. He arrested Guy Fawkes in time to foil the Gunpowder Plot. His wife, Elizabeth, was governess to King James's two youngest daughters, Mary and Sophia, both of whom died in infancy. Knyvett's local memorial is the school he founded in Stanwell and his magnificent tomb in Stanwell Church. He was representative of many courtiers who made their homes in the area when the court was more frequently at Windsor.

After Knyvett's death, Sir Francis Leigh, a Surrey gentleman who had land at Addington and Puttenham, acquired the manor. By his marriage to Elizabeth, daughter and heiress of William Minterne of Hall Place, Thorpe (and lord of Thorpe manor), Leigh ensured that his son, Wolley, had a good inheritance. Later Wolley Leigh was prominent in leading local opposition to Charles I's reintroduction of forest law in the 1630s. After the restoration, the manor was sold twice, first to Sir William Drake (1669) and then to Richard Taylor whose descendants continued to live at Knowle Green until the end of the 19th century.

There was another estate in Staines that had not been part of the abbey's lands. This was Grovebarns. It may have originated in a hide of land whose ownership was disputed in the 14th century (Susan Reynolds, *V.C.H.* iii). It consisted of 72 acres at Knowle Green and other land scattered among the open fields of Staines and Laleham. The Knowles family held the freehold in the 16th century and built up the estate to 200 acres. Thomas, who inherited in 1617, was a contemporary of Andrew Durdant and, like his neighbour, held the office of churchwarden. In 1634, William Knowles sold Grovebarns. It passed through many different owners, as it had in the 15th century, seldom being retained in the same family for even two generations.

Manorial lands and titles were not the only rich pickings to be had by speculators, whether courtiers, shrewd local gentlemen and yeomen or prosperous London citizens. There were also the rectories, vicarages and their tithes, which had been part of the endowments of the monasteries. The rectory in Staines, which yielded income from the great tithe, initially remained in the Crown's possession. After 1601, it passed through several hands, probably speculators hoping to make a quick profit. In 1621, it came into the ownership of William Stidolf, whose family had already bought the site (as distinct from the lordship) of Egham. Like the Durdants, the Stidolfs were local. Thomas Bartholomew, a member of another local family, bought the rectory in 1631 and it continued to be in the family's possession until 1725.

Egham's post-dissolution history parallels that of Staines in many respects. By 1543, the manor was in the hands of the Crown, and then granted on a lease first to a courtier, Sir Anthony Browne, and then to 'Mr Fitzwilliams'. Both men had responsibility for the preservation of the deer, Browne being keeper of the forest. This Fitzwilliam may have been an illegitimate son of one of Henry VIII's boon companions, William Fitzwilliam, Earl of Southampton. Sir Anthony Browne was the Earl's heir-at-law and half brother. (His son, another Anthony Browne, became Viscount Montague in 1554.) The lease remained in the Fitzwilliam family until the end of the century. It was then granted first to Prince Henry, James I's eldest son and, after his premature death, to Prince Charles. It became part of Henrietta Maria's jointure when she married Charles.

Somewhat confusingly the distinction was made between the lordship of the manor and the actual site. Queen Elizabeth granted the latter to William Greene, son of Michael of Milton Place. In 1587 it was sold to Thomas Stidolf (brother of William, who held Staines rectory) and inherited by his son, Francis. It remained in the family until the early 18th century.

The economic fall out of the king's seizure of monastic property obviously provided opportunities for gain for those well placed to take advantage. For more modest leaseholders the consequences were mixed. There was the uncertainty of new masters and new officials running the manorial court. One good outcome was that existing leases, most being long-term ones, were protected by statute. It was valuable to have a long lease when inflation persisted for the remainder of the century. It meant that rents were pegged while prices rose. On the negative side was the Crown's tendency to grant reversions of leases as a way of attempting to satisfy as many people as possible. It had the virtue of costing the Crown little but it forced down the value of the lease to the current holder. Those who could afford it bought up any reversion on their property. One example is that of Francis Stidolf, in 1607, who felt compelled to buy up the reversion on his property before it reduced further in value.

Copyholders fared better. They continued to have the conditions on which they held confirmed and supported by the manorial court. They had security of tenure, the right of inheritance (subject to paying a fine and taking an oath of allegiance) and, if a dispute arose, they had the assurance of a judgement by a jury of their neighbours. In most practical ways they were as good as freeholders.

Society appeared to become more fluid as new owners seized the opportunities offered by the market in former monastic land. It was nothing new, but the influx of more courtiers and speculators was on a

34   Egham Lych Gate. It was discovered in a private garden and recognised as the porch of the medieval church.

35 The *Catherine Wheel Inn*, the largest in Egham and leased by Chertsey Abbey in 1508 for 200 years. The abbey's dissolution in 1537 did not negate the lease.

larger scale. The greater use of Windsor by the court may also have contributed to the increase in gentlemen of the royal household establishing themselves in the area. Earlier in the 16th century John Yerly, a gentleman of the royal household, leased Milton Place in Egham from Corpus Christi College, Oxford. It was then leased to the king's physician, Sir William Buttes. Later on, another lessee, Michael Grene, was described as 'servaunte to the Queen's Matie'. Archbishop Warham's brother, Hugh, acquired land in Egham that included the manor of Imworth, the site of Great Fosters, 100 acres at Barneswyke (which may be on Egham Hill) and two farms in Staines, one of which was Bridge Foot. His son, Sir William, received a knighthood at Mary's coronation. He became involved in a complex of lawsuits relating to his land and fell into the hands of an associate, Jasper Palmer, goldsmith and moneylender.

Another London goldsmith, William Denham, leased Waltam Place in Thorpe in 1567, following a well-worn path from the city to a country estate within a day's travelling from London. In the 14th century Nicholas Brembre, grocer and lord mayor, had acquired land in Staines, Stanwell, Yeoveney and Egham that, after his death, eventually reverted to the Crown and was vested in Westminster Abbey. Denham's son became a distinguished judge on the King's Bench and leased the Egham manor of Imworth, where he built a new manor house. He married the widow of Richard Kellifet, another member of the royal household, with an estate in Egham at Rusham.

The confident prosperity of these men, who had profited from the market in land after the dissolution of the monasteries, conceals the turbulence of the 30 years from the first meeting of the Reformation parliament in 1529 to the accession of Elizabeth in November 1558. The rebellions, part religious, part economic, which punctuated the period did not reach the Staines area but ripples were felt. In 1536-7, risings in Lincolnshire and Yorkshire, aimed at defending and restoring the smaller monasteries, evoked sympathy. In Windsor a priest expressed sympathy with the northern rebels in the Pilgrimage of Grace by encouraging support 'to defend God's quarrel'.

In the summer of 1549 a number of revolts erupted against the Protestant programme of Protector Somerset. The nearest outbreak was Oxfordshire, where ringleaders were dealt with as traitors and several priests were hanged from their church towers. More serious was a rising in the South-West that besieged Exeter and threatened a march on London. The constable and churchwardens of Staines were ordered to intercept such a move by pulling down the bridge.

There was a strong reaction. A petition went before the Protector's Council. It stated that the inhabitants of Staines 'have received command from the Lord Protector to pull down Staines bridge to safeguard the realm from enemies, which will be the utter undoing of the town and its surroundings'. It continued with a mixture of defiance and compliance: 'The bridge still stands: the town has promised to send out a scout to spy any army coming that way and prays for further orders.'

The sense of alarm in the neighbourhood was conveyed in other reports from key men in the areas thought to be on the route of the rebels. Henry Polsted, whose loyalty was rewarded a year later with land in Egham and Thorpe, reported to William Cecil that large areas of Surrey including the Chertsey area were 'weak of worthy men'. He needed sound JPs and a secure gaol. The Earl of Arundel, reporting to Sir William Petrie on the general state of security in Surrey, wrote,

'These parts remain as well as may be in a quivering quiet. The honest promise to serve the king; the rest, I trust, will follow.' It was touch and go.

During July, the court moved to Windsor where the leading gentry and nobility of the southern counties were summoned with the request to bring 'able horsemen and footmen from your tenants, servants and others' and their equipment. In reality it was a muster of forces in case the worst happened. To general relief in the area, it did not. The rebels failed to take Exeter and were defeated after a siege of six weeks.

Just as the bridge had a strategic importance for the government in its concern to defend London, so it had a key economic value to Staines and the neighbourhood. Its maintenance, therefore, was vital to many groups and interests. It seems that, over the centuries, good intentions to keep the bridge in repair were numerous; effectiveness, however, was rare.

The Crown took a keen but sporadic interest. In the 13th century there were several grants of pontage to the bridge wardens. These allowed the collection of tolls from which the bridge was to be repaired. The grants continued at intervals into the 15th century but the system appears to have been very haphazard with tolls seldom raising the funds needed. In a somewhat desperate effort to increase income, the bridge wardens were allowed to beg for alms from travellers. It seems not to have been very effective and it was, moreover, rather unfair of the 'authorities' to compete with regular beggars who relied on the alms of travellers for their survival.

Local people occasionally left money for the bridge and the road approaching it on the Surrey side. John Hanhampstede, already mentioned for his gifts to Egham Church, also left £10 for mending the way from Staines to Bakehamcross and 13s. 4d. for mending the way from Rushamsgate to Prytewelhill (Prune Hill).

The will of Robert Wade, a merchant tailor of London, who moved to Egham in 1525, gave 'to the maintenance of the highway that stretcheth from the Kateryne Whele at Egham to Old Brigge towards Staines, 40s, if they will make it, to be paid when it is made and done'. It sounds as though there was some lack of confidence in the fulfilment of the bequest.

The whole matter was put on a firmer basis by an Act of 1509. This appointed wardens with statutory power to raise tolls and to be answerable to Chancery. There were still frequent disputes between Staines and Egham over responsibility for bridge maintenance and excuses to do nothing. In 1597 the terms of the 1509 Act were reinforced with the appointment of two additional toll collectors who had to be from Egham. The Egham lobby had obviously been busy. In an effort to improve administration, a penalty of £10 was set for misappropriation of tolls.

In spite of best efforts, the problems of the bridge continued. In 1618 the Lord Chancellor Francis Bacon wrote to the Lord Mayor of London about the problems. Tolls were alleged to amount to £24 but the cost of repairs was estimated at £1,000, presumably the result of a long backlog of repairs. Even a general collection throughout Middlesex and counties west of the bridge failed to raise sufficient for the necessary repairs.

Staines also had responsibility for the bridge over the River Colne known as Longford Bridge. In 1612 the churchwardens Andrew Durdant and Robert Weekes were indicted at the Middlesex Quarter Sessions because the community had failed to carry out repairs. It was a story that ran and ran until a new bridge was planned almost 200 years later.

Chapter Five

Parish Government and Civil War

An Egham will of 1592 contains a remarkable bequest. Richard Atwick, whose family was certainly in the locality in the late 14th century, endowed a sermon to be preached in Staines on 20 Good Fridays, adding 'if this religion now professed, continewe, or else not'. There is

no doubt about his Protestantism, nor about his pessimism. At a greater distance in time from the turmoil of the middle years of the 16th century, such uncertainty seems to us unnecessary, even a perverse misreading of Elizabeth's reign. It is, however, a salutary reminder that history always has the dubious

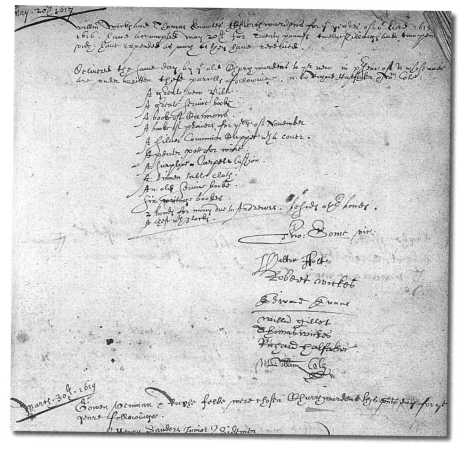

36 Staines' churchwardens' book showing an inventory taken in 1616. The list includes a great new Bible (the King James Bible, 1611) and a book of prayers to be used to commemorate the foiling of the 1605 Gunpowder Plot.

37 Fines levied in 1656 by the church-wardens for inappropriate behaviour; for example, Thomas Stanny for being drunk and Mr Collins 'for drawing with a wagon on the Lord's Day'.

benefit of hindsight. Coming from a strongly Protestant family, Richard hardly dared believe that a plateau of stability had been reached. But this was to prove so, as James I succeeded Elizabeth peacefully, ended war with Spain and set about carving his name in history by commissioning a new translation of the Bible from the original languages.

In 1611, the churchwardens of Staines made one of their periodic efforts to keep their records better. That year they listed the church's valuable property, which included the newly issued King James Bible. The next inventory did not appear until 1617, perhaps prompted by the appointment of a new vicar, Dr Some. The following composite list illustrates the paucity of the church's possessions and is a reminder of what had been lost at the time of the Reformation: silver cup and cover; pewter jug; a great new Bible; communion cloth; carpet and cushion for pulpit; surplice; old service book; book of sermons; book of prayers; chest to lock them in with their locks and keys; five writing books. The chalice and jug were all that remained of the elaborate furnishings of the pre-Reformation altars. Only the surplice remained of the priest's vestments. The old service book was probably the Elizabethan Book of Common Prayer (1559) supplemented since 1605 with a book of prayers to mark King James' escape from the Gunpowder plotters in 1605. The book of sermons is a reminder that Protestantism was a religion of the Word as read in the Bible and heard in the sermon. The furnishings of the pulpit always seem to be of importance to ensure the parson's comfort in an unheated and ill-repaired church.

The churchwardens were elected annually at the parish vestry meeting, together with other key officials who constituted the local government. Attendances at the vestry ranged between 10 and 20 in the 1620s, so they were hardly representative of the community. The same family names recur over the years, usually belonging to men of some substance, gentlemen such as Andrew Durdant and Richard Halfaker, yeoman farmers, craftsmen and traders. Almost all

showed some degree of literacy and signed their names. It may have been a sign of wider interest and participation in the 1650s that the numbers attending increased, but so did those making their marks rather than signing their names.

The churchwardens were the guardians of the church, responsible for maintaining its fabric (although the vicar was responsible for the chancel), for raising the church rate and for reporting twice a year to the archdeacon on breaches of behaviour that came within the jurisdiction of church courts. They were empowered to make presentiments on recusancy, non-attendance at church, adultery, drunkenness and behaving badly

38 Monument to Sir John Denham in Egham Church.

39 Sir John Denham's monument to his two wives in Egham Church. The small figure is Sir John, the poet and royalist, who spent many years in exile from 'parliamentary' Egham.

in church. They were often charged with extra duties such as administering and accounting for legacies to the community. Two such legacies were those of Richard Halfaker and Nathaniel Lone. Halfaker left £4 income annually from his house, the *George*, to be paid to a teacher to teach four poor children the Psalter and Testament. Here is Protestantism in action, asserting the necessity of informed belief. When needed, the churchwardens were to appoint a new teacher. A little more onerous in its execution was Lone's bequest (1625) of 52s. annually from his land in Little Old Bailey in London to provide 12d. worth of bread

each Sunday for distribution to the poor. (By 1916, Lone's capital sum had risen to £996 19s. 1d.) Halfaker also left £5 for building a steeple; it was timely for the rebuilding, in 1631, of the church tower.

Walter Holt and William Gillett (1628) each made small bequests to support poor apprentices by equipping them with a new set of clothes and paying a master initially to take them on for an apprenticeship. In 1652, the churchwardens were unsure what to do with Holt's legacy. The paperwork, as often happened, was mislaid. The Holt family were established in Staines in the 16th century and at least two other members held office after Walter's death. Thomas was churchwarden in 1648, having already been an overseer of the poor, and William Holt the younger was a sidesman (assistant to the churchwardens) in 1659.

In 1627, Judge Denham founded Egham's first regular charity for the poor. The recipients were to be housed and provided with 12d. each Sunday and an annual set of clothing: a cloth gown at Michaelmas and, at Whitsuntide, a smock, a pair of stockings and a pair of shoes. Any surplus was to go on repairs to the houses and fuel. Denham's Royalist son neglected the charity and left the area. Turner comments tartly that, in spite of his debts, he managed to continue living in comfort.

In many parishes, the churchwardens doubled as overseers of the poor. This may, in part, have been of necessity for want of candidates or volunteers for the post, but there was good sense as well in this arrangement. Many issues overlapped, as illustrated in both Staines and Egham, in the administering of charities. However, Staines achieved a separation of office-holders even though there are many instances of

churchwardens stepping in and using church rates to help parishioners in distress. A special note in the churchwardens' accounts for 1621 appears to be a reminder about the method of collecting the poor rate. It was to be paid quarterly 'in church to the churchwardens and ourselves' the following Sunday after the clerk had announced the rate due in church.

In practice, the officials seldom lived up to the modest standard of efficiency that this note suggests. For some years the accounts are blank, for example, for most of the 1620s. Not until 1637 are there any indications of how money was disbursed. During the 1640s the entries are more regular and more accurate but not always correct. In 1643 the clerk recorded his dissatisfaction with the state of affairs. The churchwardens, Mr Wickes (Thomas, later referred to as Captain) and Thomas Gally, 'melted lead on the north aisle and did account for none of it neither is any set into this church book as it ought'.

This small spat was an indication of the tensions caused by the Civil War. Wickes appeared as a leading force in the parish

40   The Place, Egham, built by Sir John Denham on the site of the old Imworth manor house. Today, the police station stands in what had been the manor's grounds.

giving his support to Parliament. By 1649, it seems that matters had settled: Wickes and the other churchwarden, Haxle, accounted properly for the lead (presumably used to aid the Parliamentary troops who occupied Staines in 1643) and also for 52s. owing to Dr Some.

The vicar of Staines from 1616 was Thomas Some (Soame) who had been a fellow of Peterhouse and became a Doctor of Divinity in 1627. He held several appointments, being a Canon of St Paul's (1616) and a Canon of Windsor (1622). In 1640 he was also vicar of Twickenham. Although he was rarely present at vestry meetings – he signed in 1617 and 1640 – he probably resided for some periods in the parish. Three daughters and a son were born in Staines between 1621 and 1632. He probably removed himself from Staines in 1640, perhaps to Twickenham. There, in 1643, he was accused of bowing to the altar and for causing further offence for giving thanks for the king's victory at Brentford. In 1646 he was deprived of his livings, spent a period in prison and then allowed to move to Oxford where the king had his headquarters and where he was granted a living within Royalist-held territory. In 1642, Richard Eburne appeared as 'minister', a puritan term, and from 1650 Gabriel Price was acting as minister, the vicarage having been sequestered by Parliament. (Edward Calamy, the contemporary biographer of the ministers who were removed in 1660 and 1662, dated Price's ministry from 1654.) Price favoured a Presbyterian form of Church government. The removal of the font indicated radical beliefs and the reglazing of windows and the repairing and the painting of the chancel suggest that images surviving since the Reformation were purged.

Other signs of radicalism were the vigorous actions taken by the churchwardens to fulfil their duties in policing the morals of the parishioners. Thomas Haxle was convicted of drunkenness in 1656 for which he gave 5s. for the clerk to distribute to six poor widows. Mr Collins (probably a yeoman farmer from his title) was fined 20s. for using his wagon on a Sunday while Mr Hopkins, indicted by Roger Living, was fined 5s. for travelling on a Sunday.

Under Cromwell's rule, the levying of Church rates became compulsory as part of a policy of making the administration of local government more effective. In particular this improved help for the poor. The overseers helped orphaned children by paying for their care, often by a widow, and then helping to fund an apprenticeship. Those who were unable to work because of illness or an accident received stipends. During 1655 there were six people being helped by the payment of 6s. a week. The widow Teddar looked after two parish children, receiving £9 9s. for 42 weeks and a further 2s. 6d. to provide them with shoes. The poor rate in Staines raised about £40 in the 1640s and 1650s but by the end of the century it had risen to £200 annually. Payment was the landlord's responsibility, and the rate was based on property. At the wealthier end of the scale Andrew Durdant paid £5, William Lidgold (who leased the parsonage) £2, Captain Wickes and Mr Holt £2 10s. while John the Hatter was assessed at 8d. The poor rates were presented annually for approval by the JPs. This probably explains why they were less haphazard than the books of the churchwardens.

The role of JPs in the community increased during the 17th century. In part this was the result of more government activity, in particular to control poverty and its perceived connection with disorder. In addition, the manorial courts had lost much of their effectiveness and disappeared in many places, although not in Egham. The local official with power of arrest was

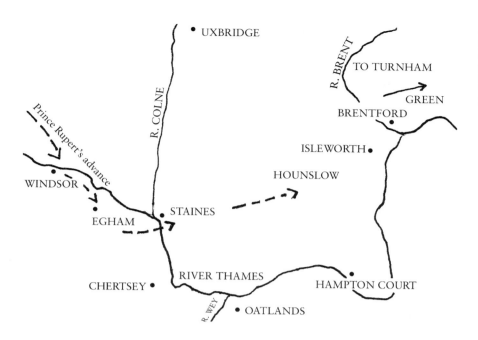

41 Sketch map of the area showing the site of the major Civil War events in 1642.

the constable, appointed by the vestry and able to appoint deputies. It was usual for a leading inhabitant to be constable and use deputies to deal with offenders and any unpleasantness in the streets or around the town's fields. The system was open to abuse and inefficiency.

One 15th-century example illustrates this. A couple, Simon and Joan Flegg, were arrested as absconding debtors by the Egham constable prior to being taken to London, where they claimed they could prove their innocence. A certain Thomas Totnam, claiming to be constable of Staines, offered to help his 'colleague' by escorting them to London. Once in Staines, the couple were in the jurisdiction of the Abbot of Westminster, the Egham constable was rendered legally powerless and Totnam was revealed as an impersonator.

Horse-stealing was one of the most common crimes and was usually committed by people from outside the neighbourhood.

Being on a major road into London, both Staines and Egham suffered from such thefts from travellers lodging at the many inns. If caught and found guilty, the penalty was hanging. Travellers were also in danger from personal assault and robbery on lonely, notorious stretches of road nearby. Two of these were Hounslow Heath and the road towards Bagshot Heath. There was concern at Christmas time 1604 when an assault on a traveller resulted in his murder near Windlesham. He had been robbed of his cloak, dagger, rapier and £10 in money. The attacker was not captured.

The sub-constables in Staines could easily find themselves in trouble. In 1612, one was ordered to answer to the justices in Brentford, having allowed a sheep thief to escape. When James Perry was sub-constable he was assaulted trying to arrest George Leese, an upholsterer. A shoemaker nearby was asked to help; he refused and, in turn, was arrested. In court he refused to give surety for his good behaviour. 'The Justices might commit him if they would for he would put in no sureties.' Clearly he thought he had no obligation to help the sub-constables.

The peace of the area was much more seriously disturbed when the movement of troops around the country led to demands for billeting. In 1626 when the king's favourite, the Duke of Buckingham, was leading badly organised attacks on Spain, he needed a troop of 400 to march into Kent. They had to be quartered en route in Staines. The deputy lieutenants of Middlesex were alarmed and appealed for help and instructions: 'To-morrow night there will be as many more.' The quartermaster of one of the regiments wrote to Sir Francis Darcy appealing for money to pay his soldiers and for carts and hackneys to transport the equipment and allow them to leave Staines the next day. Compensation for the townsfolk, who had been compelled to provide bread and board as well as fodder for the horses, looked unlikely. Only one day earlier the government learned that 700 men, the remnant of Buckingham's disastrous raid on Cadiz, were encamped awaiting their pay off. There was no money available.

When Civil War broke out in 1642 the problem of billeting was much greater and prolonged. Staines was a western outpost of

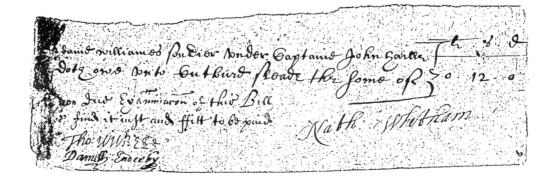

42 (*top left*) Notes claiming payment for the billeting of troops in Staines during the Civil War. These are from a collection of 101 such bills, mostly counter-signed to authorise payment by Sergeant Major Nathaniel Whetham. The first is a list of Captain Browne's men owing for their 'dyet' to Robartte Cutler of the *White Horse*.

43 (*middle left*) Three soldiers billeted on Daniel Enderby owe £4.

44 (*bottom left*) The churchwardens signed as correct a soldier's I.O.U. for 12 shillings.

45 (*right*) Debts for hay and oats supplied by Mr Durdant, lord of the manor of Yeoveney to Captain Nutwell's horses at the *George* and meals at 4d. each for five soldiers over three weeks.

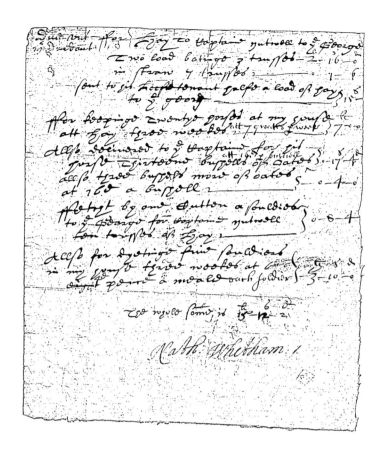

London. At the outbreak of war, the king had left his capital where Parliament had control. After the first clash in the Midlands at Edge Hill, the Royalist forces attempted to retake London. Parliament acted quickly in securing Windsor Castle so that Prince Rupert had to turn aside and pause in Egham. It was well-sited for crossing the Thames and confronting any attack from Londoners. It also had plenty of inns with accommodation for Prince Rupert's cavalry. The Spanish Ambassador made this strategic assessment.

There was a brief delay while negotiations for peace took place at Colnbrook. The king was anxious to have the Parliamentary forces out of Windsor but preferred to 'talk' them out rather than attempt a siege. When the talks failed – it was suggested at the time that the king was not really serious about peace negotiations – Rupert returned to Egham. He knew a large Parliamentary force under Essex was at Brentford. Under cover of night and fog he crossed Staines Bridge, surprised Essex by the suddenness of his attack and inflicted heavy casualties. He seized valuable stores, eight pieces of artillery and then sacked the place.

The London-trained bands, in effect the capital's territorial army, marched out from London for the first time ever to try to stop Rupert's advance. They prepared to take their stand at Turnham Green. But Rupert did not attack. He withdrew to join the main Royalist forces on having news of defections to Parliament that enabled his enemy to take Kingston Bridge. The King, meanwhile, went to the royal palace at Oatlands. But it was an area unsuited to sustain a large number of troops so they withdrew to Oxford.

During three tense November days, the population of Staines must have held its breath. The incident at Turnham Green, where the armies confronted each other but did not fight, was a turning point in the war. The king lost the only real chance he had of regaining his capital. Staines narrowly missed becoming a battleground. Nevertheless, it remained a war zone. It was an ideal camping ground for Parliamentary troops at various stages of the war, moving west to the siege of Basing House, gathering to go to the relief of Gloucester and then, in 1644, going to help repulse the king's forces after the second battle of Newbury. On this occasion there was a great fear that London would again need defending as in 1642, and Staines was the rendezvous for Parliamentary troops gathering in its defence.

For the people of Staines and others in West Middlesex, this meant 'free quarter' for the troops. Normally the soldiers had not been paid and, as in 1626, their officers had no money. This situation produced a deep sense of grievance, which found expression in a petition to Parliament. The people of Staines complained of being 'rendered no better than mere conquered slaves' and having to endure soldiers 'like so many Egyptian locusts so long upon us'. The committee at Derby House directing the war ordered the Committee for the Army 'to be careful to pay the forces of the Army that they be not burdensome to the country where they are now quartered'. A series of instructions was sent to the captain in charge at Staines.

'You will see by the enclosed complaint how the town of Staines is burdened by a troop taking free quarter ... We desire that they be paid and have orders to pay their quarters for the ease and content of the country.'

The details of the burden emerge from 101 notes that were claims submitted by individuals for payment. The churchwardens, Thomas Wickes and Daniel Enderby, authenticated some. All social grades were caught up in billeting. In April 1643, Enderby had endured three soldiers for 10 weeks; James Clarke, the constable claimed £6; Thomas Newbery claimed £26 16s. 4d.; Lettice Smith, widow, claimed £4 15s. 6d. in 1642 and later £9 4s. 4d. for six of Captain Brown's soldiers. Mr Durdant provided for 20 horses at Yeoveney Manor for three weeks and also sent hay and oats to Captain Nutwell at the *George*. Innkeepers at the *Angel* and the *White Horse* were others submitting large claims. It appears that there were standard charges for bed and board at 3s. or 4s. a week. Many of these debts would have been crippling to ordinary folk.

There were similar claims from Egham. Again it was inn holders and yeoman farmers, those best placed to provide for mounted troops, who fared the worst. James Guy, innholder, had supplied sheep, butter, wine, beer, wood and had household goods damaged. At various times in 1643 he had kept 459 horses under guard, grazing at Egham Hill for which, at 4d. a head, he was owed £7 13s. Double that amount was owed by 'diverse other soldiers which would not tell their names but called for meate and drink saieing they would pay afterwards but denied'. Another innholder, John Geary, was owed £38 for billeting William Waller's troops for eight weeks. John Fabian, a prosperous gentleman farmer at Rusham, had supplied hoggs (sheep) and quartering at a cost of £60, while his neighbour, Richard

46 Churchwardens' book showing the signature of Gabriel Price, the intruded minister.

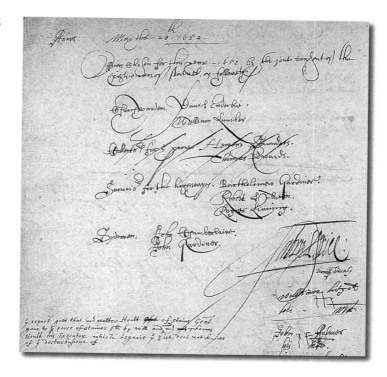

Mountain, had £500 worth of bills, bonds and household goods stolen.

Sympathisers with Parliament and Royalists appear to have suffered without distinction. Leading Royalists left if they could and joined the King early in the war at Oxford. Those who remained trimmed their sails and eventually co-operated in the administration of the district. Many Egham farmers co-operated practically in sending horses to help at the siege of Basing and in making loans to Parliament in the form of money and plate. These included the minister, William Reyner (Rayner), James Guy, William Kirkham and Daniel Weeks.

Royalists who fled were penalised. Denham (the poet) was already in debt when he left his wife to manage as best she could. He forfeited all but one-fifth of his estates (which were chiefly in Essex). His wife was eventually allowed to leave for London after she complained of her treatment. She had

many times had 20 or 30 troops billeted at her Imworth manor house, had 14 of her horses commandeered and her husband's tenants had been ordered to withhold their rents by the Committee of Sequestrations. Only in 1655 was Denham allowed to return to Egham, answerable for his good behaviour to Reyner and then, in 1656, allowed to return to practise the law in London.

Denham's main creditor in Egham was John Thynne (a cousin of the Thynnes of Longleat). By 1647 he had taken possession of the lease of the manor of Egham and the Denham house at Imworth. Thynne co-operated with the new Parliamentary authorities and, although a Royalist sympathiser, kept his new acquisitions.

Sir Henry Spiller of Laleham was unfortunate to be in the West Country taking the waters for his health when the war broke out. He was taken prisoner by Parliamentary troops in Gloucester and charged as a

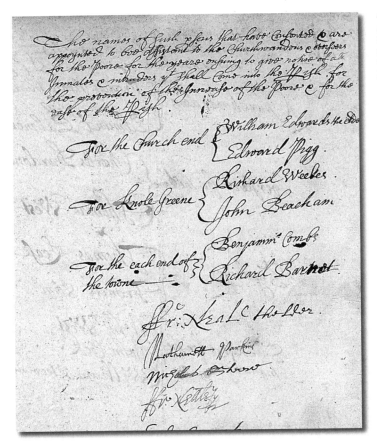

47 Churchwardens' book, 1660. Appointments made by the annual vestry meeting showing, for the first time, representation of districts or 'wards' of the town: Church End, Each End, Knowle Green.

delinquent for residing in the king's quarters. His fine was £8,961, reduced by £300 because he was committed to a marriage settlement for his granddaughter. His discharge from delinquency was delayed partly because he died during the legal process. His widow achieved discharge only in 1653 and then lost two-thirds of her claim because she was a recusant.

By 1645, the war had entered a decisive phase. The Parliamentary armies were reorganised into the New Model Army, which was better paid and relied, at least in theory, on recruits rather than conscripts. The problem of quarters for troops was not entirely overcome but it probably diminished because the new administration was better

at tax-gathering and soldiers were therefore more likely to have been paid than in the early days of the war.

However, Staines remained vulnerable because of large numbers of soldiers on its doorstep. Hounslow Heath was the rendezvous for London recruits. Early in 1645, there were large camps nearby while peace negotiations were held at Uxbridge. These failed and peace was illusory for the next two years. The king remained intransigent while divisions among the victors increased. During an attempted coup in London, in 1647, when the more radical elements in the army tried to seize power, Staines was once again a rendezvous before the final stage of the dissidents' march on the capital.

Chapter Six

THE RIVERSIDE ECONOMY: THE SEVENTEENTH CENTURY

The unpleasant consequences of the Civil War did not vanish quickly. Economically Staines suffered from the destruction of the bridge at some stage in the war and the long delay in rebuilding it fully. The menace of billeting and the threat caused by the proximity of troops were other wartime features that remained. The quartering of troops when the king was at Windsor was normal. In June 1679, the Duke of Monmouth asked that four companies of footguards march to Windsor to attend the king 'till further order'. At the same time, two companies of Coldstream Guards were sent to Windsor. When not on duty, their billets were in Egham, Staines and other places nearby. The growth in road traffic in the years after the Restoration gave rise to more inns in Egham and Staines. Consequently, both places had exactly the requirements for lodging soldiers and stabling horses. In April 1680, the quartermaster was ordered to Staines and Egham 'where our Horse Guards lodge when we keep our Court at Windsor'.

Often the royal entourage passed through Staines when returning to London from Windsor. On these occasions the church bells had to be rung and the ringers paid in cash and beer. The activities on Hounslow Heath, long used as a rendezvous and occasional camp for the army, became alarming during the brief reign of James II (1685-8). In 1686, after defeating the Duke of Monmouth's rebellion, James kept his army intact and established a great camp on Hounslow Heath. There, on 30 June, he reviewed 13,000 troops and in July sent another 4,000 mounted troops to gather on Staines' meadows to escort the Queen from Windsor to Hounslow. There were ugly rumours that the king intended to impose his will on the country, turning it by force of arms and by subverting the constitution into a Catholic state.

Macaulay described the intimidating camp with its thousands of troops and impressive artillery. 'The Londoners saw this great force assembled in their neighbourhood with a terror which familiarity soon diminished. The camp presented the appearance of a vast fair. Mingled with musketeers and dragoons, a multitude of fine gentlemen and ladies from Soho Square, sharpers and painted women from Whitefriars … pedlars, orange-girls, mischievous apprentices and gaping clowns were constantly passing and repassing through the long line of tents … In truth the place was merely a gay suburb of the capital.'

When, in July 1688, news reached the camp that the seven bishops accused of seditious libel had been acquitted, a great roar of approval arose from the soldiers. It told James that he could not rely on his army's loyalty. Within weeks, he fled to France rather

48 Duncroft House. One of Staines' very few old buildings, the house dates from the mid-17th century. Its rarity, therefore, has given rise to improbable stories of connection to King John and his residency there before meeting the barons.

than face the Prince of Orange's invasion. Once again, as in 1549, Staines was defiant when ordered to dismantle its newly restored bridge. William of Orange's speed saved the bridge from destruction and the bridge masters from punishment.

The value of the bridge and of uninterrupted river transport grew during the 17th century as inland trade expanded and with it the wealth of the country. The responsibility for maintaining this highway rested with the City of London, which had purchased royal rights over the river from Richard I. The city's specific jurisdiction was traditionally claimed upstream as far as Staines and marked by the Boundary or London Stone. The date on the stone, 1285 (reportedly, in 1811, 1280), marks the setting up of the stone rather than the origin of the city's jurisdiction. During the 13th century there was already river traffic between London and Oxford even though there were many obstacles – lack of towing paths, shallows, weirs and annual flooding – to be overcome. Weirs continued to be a problem,

often legislated against as an intrusion of the private property claims of anglers and millers against a public right of way. The laws were as often as not flouted. Henry IV granted a weir at Strand on the Green in 1411 but the city authorities managed to remove one granted by Edward IV. Elizabeth's governments seem to have been more aware of the importance of unimpeded passage on the river and conducted enquiries in 1580 and 1590 into the number of weirs in existence.

Conditions must have improved greatly in subsequent decades. One piece of evidence is the publication in 1637 of Taylor's *Carriers Compendium*, which was a timetable of regular freight sailings up and down the river. Michael Robbins described it as an early *Bradshaw*: 'Great boats that do carry passengers … and go away upon Tuesdays and Thursdays'. By the end of the century, these barges were so regular that the Egham diarist, Henry Strode, could tell he had arrived in Staines by midday because the barge to London had not left. In 1641 Taylor commented that the 'River Thames is by the care and providence of the Lord Mayor, well conserved and kept from impediments of stops, weares, sand beds and other hinderances of passage of eyther Boates or Barges'. Upstream, Taylor also claimed there were almost no stoppages. This was good news for the prosperity of Staines.

The little town suffered a setback with the damage done to the bridge during the Civil War. For a period, a ferry was used to cross the river and was essential to transport the barge horses from the point where the towpath on the Middlesex bank ended (the 'shooting off place') to its continuation someway upstream on the Surrey side. The Grand Duke of Tuscany, Cosmo III, wrote in his *Travels* of reaching Egham from Basingstoke on Palm Sunday, 1669. He stayed overnight and then 'crossed the Thames by a wooden bridge a mile from Egham' where the river was shallow. From this, one might conclude that the bridge had been restored, but it may only have been a temporary repair.

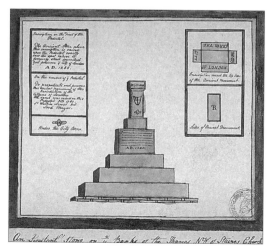

49 London Stone repaired and erected on a new pedestal in 1781. Camden referred to the Stone, its date, 1285, and its inscription 'God preserve the City of London'. It was a reminder of London's dependence on the River Thames as a trade route.

The disruption caused tolls to rise. In 1672 tolls on passenger boats rowing upstream from London to Maidenhead were 7d. to pass under Staines Bridge instead of the traditional 4d., which had been charged at least up to 1640. Fred Thacker (*The Thames Highway*, vol. II) quotes a damaged document on the subject: 'Staines Bridge being broken downe in tyme of the late unhappy Warrs and the Bridge Masters finding a fferry Boate to carry over the Horses … was the onely and chief cause of the Bargemasters beinge raysed to pay 7d a Barge.' But there was another reason for the toll increase: the decayed condition of the Egham causeway and its urgent need of repair.

Other improvements were made during the 17th century. These include regular dredging and, after 1636, against much opposition the introduction of pound locks. An early one in 1623 at Henley had made a great improvement to navigation and contributed to the area becoming a major source of corn for London.

This long-term concern with Thames navigation is directly related to the phenomenal growth of London and the voracious demands of its population. It stimulated farming practice and production and effected a horticultural boom in the Thames Valley. In 1500 London had about 50,000 inhabitants and was already spilling out beyond its walls to artisan suburbs in Aldgate and Southwark. By 1600 it had 200,000 people, so, given existing high rates of mortality, which in pre-industrial times checked excessive population growth, London's growth had to look to migrants to sustain itself. In the first instance, the incomers came from areas of the country nearest London, so many workers and apprentices from the area around Staines and Egham would have been drawn into the city.

50   The Lord Mayor's visit, 1839, at London Stone. The city's assertion of its jurisdiction became an excuse for pomp and ceremony involving a river procession of livery barges accompanying the state barge of the Lord Mayor. (Copyright of Surrey History Service.)

The relative security of the many copyhold farmers in Staines and Egham (i.e. those holding land that had been part of the manors held respectively by Westminster and Chertsey Abbeys) removed one of the main obstacles to innovation. Neither was there the pressure experienced in many parts of the Midlands to enclose the old-fashioned open fields in order to raise production. Staines and Egham remained unenclosed until the 19th century. Instead, there was much experimentation with crops and methods of cultivation and plenty of land that could be taken in from waste. In Staines and probably to a lesser extent in Egham, the scattered strips of each holding across the open fields were independently cultivated, rather than following the traditional policy of common planting and rotation. Most copyholders had acquired additional land from waste that they enclosed as fields in the modern sense.

They were referred to as 'closes'. Fruit and vegetables were foremost among the crops grown for profit. Proximity to London and good transport meant they could be freshly marketed.

The old-fashioned open fields and often-wasteful scattering of the strips of an individual owner did not prevent experimentation and the introduction of a variety of crops. Often the land did not lie fallow for a season to recuperate but was planted with 'green' crops such as sainfoin, lucerne and clover. These discouraged the proliferation of weeds, some were 'fixers' of nitrogen in the soil and all could be harvested to add variety and increase the quantity of fodder for the farm animals.

Egham is fortunate in having a diarist who recorded many details of agricultural practice and social life during 1699 and spring 1700. He was Henry Strode, the

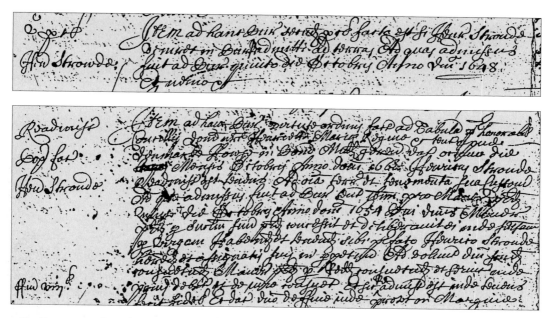

51 Two extracts from the Egham manorial court roll, 1667. The first summons the father of the diarist, Henry Strode, to be readmitted to his lands which he inherited in 1654 (not 1648 as stated). The second formally admits him, making legal a transaction carried out during Cromwell's Protectorate and regarded as illegal by the restored monarchy.

founder of a charity school and almshouses by his 1704 will. He came of an old-established Egham family: the name first appears in the 15th century and wills survive from 1569. Although illegitimate, Henry Strode's grandfather had inherited the family's copyhold land in or about 1606 when plague had wiped out the main family. The diarist was born in London and became a very wealthy wholesale wine merchant. In 1683 he inherited the Egham lands and seems to have divided his time between London and Egham. In the country, he immersed himself in the detailed management of his lands and he was not afraid to get his hands dirty. He repaired a broken ladder in the yard and put studs in the wall to hang it out of the way. In September he was up at the Brooke, on the western edge of Englefield Green, mending a hedge and the next day down in Egham at the Hummer acre (by the modern-day Tesco store) mending a broken stile. He recorded his walks across the parish and beyond (one Sunday he walked to Eton to see his plumber) and he kept a record of the daily tasks of his workmen.

The entries for August and September 1699 give a picture of the busiest time of the farming year. The main crops of barley, wheat, rye and oats had been harvested and Strode's men were busy ploughing in three widely separated parts of the parish. Strode's copyhold land totalled almost 39 acres in 34 separate pieces. Twelve of these were in the common fields; then there was a comparatively large plot of six acres at Bellfields (off the modern Wick Road at the edge of the Great Park) and several pieces of meadow in Longmead, Runnymead, Yard Mead, downstream from Bell Weir and in Thorpe Lea. It was a widely scattered holding, not very efficient by present-day

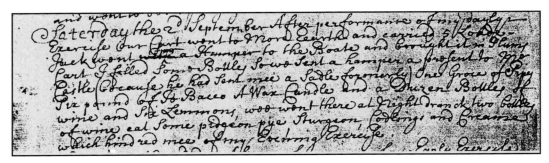

52   Extract from Henry Strode's diary, 1699.

standards but capable of producing crops for the market.

A second crop of hay, mainly clover, was taken in September from the Brooke. It took one of Strode's men two days to mow with a sickle. 'He made an end late at night.' It was left to dry for almost a week, occasionally being inspected and turned to help it to dry. After rain, which caused Strode to think his crop had been spoiled, there came a drying wind. Extra help was called out and it was with some satisfaction that they brought a load and a half down Egham Hill to the barn at the Strode farmhouse, Grovesend, near the bottom of the hill.

Although a relatively new crop, clover was being used in Surrey as early as 1670 as part of rotation schemes. It ensured a more nutritious feed for over-wintering animals and it enriched the soil. It was one of many new crops, introduced in the middle years of the 17th century, which were the subject of experimentation in Surrey. These included new varieties of grass, other legumes, madder, mulberry and tobacco. Some succeeded well in the light, poorish soils found in Staines and Egham. Farmers took the risk of trying something new because of the continuing rise in the price of food and the insatiable demand of London.

53   Strode's charity school and almshouses founded in 1704 with an endowment of £6,000. This pen-and-wash drawing, 1812, shows the building very little changed from its beginning in 1707. Almost £2,000 was invested in land in Staines as part of the charity's endowment. (Copyright of Surrey History Service.)

While the clover hay was being turned and collected, other farm helpers were collecting beans and peas. These were brought into the close next to the farmhouse to dry and after three days in the sun they were thrashed. To Strode's indignation 'the Beanes wee had sett in the close to dry, somebody had stolen four Bundles of them last night and it was well I brought them in for it raigned the Night following'. Turnips were sown in the Hummer acre for a late crop; some were already in the ground, being regularly hoed. Turnips had been used primarily for the table and only later became an important animal feed during the winter months. It seems that the local practice was to leave the last ones in the ground over winter and then use them when fodder was scarce in the late winter.

The light soils near the Thames proved well-suited to growing vegetables, which had become a fashionable item of diet in London after the Civil War. It was a fashion that gained momentum as greater French influence was felt after the Restoration in 1660. There were commercial nurseries for fruit trees and the production of seed in Thameside villages such as Battersea, Putney and Isleworth. All this enterprise helped feed London and those gardens nearest the city benefited from the manure that London produced.

With timetabled barges plying to Staines and upstream, similar opportunities opened up for marketing surplus produce from Staines and Egham farmers. There were plenty of gardens, orchards and closes that the enterprising could use. Even the main streets were punctuated by gardens or closes and were not solidly lined by houses. Deeds that have survived from the 17th century frequently mention gardens and orchards of a quarter or half-acre associated with the main house.

54 The Market House, Staines, dating from c.1660. It stood on the left of the High Street at the approach to the bridge. Its open ground floor gave shelter to traders. Market day was Friday, but the original grant in 1218 had declared market day to be Sunday. (Copyright of Surrey History Service.)

In 1626 Thomas (later Captain) Wickes sold a house, orchard and garden adjoining Frogpole Common in Staines. The property was typical of many in the two villages. A century later Henry Herring, a rich London financier with an Egham link through his mother and uncle Henry Strode, was busy buying and selling similar messuages in Egham, all with accompanying orchards and gardens. They were clearly still very desirable pieces of real estate for a shrewd investor.

Barley was an important commodity in the district and widely grown as a cash crop for producing beer. Surpluses of wheat, often mixed with rye as maslin, and oats for fodder were other crops of the open fields. Some of the surpluses were marketed in Staines at the Friday market and the larger growers might use the main corn market of the area, which was the one in Brentford. More likely, the local surpluses would be bought by a dealer and traded on at Brentford.

Everyone drank beer. Many households made their own, as did Strode, light and low in alcohol, known as 'small beer'. But there was also a huge demand for beer produced by brewers. It was a safer and more palatable drink than water. Again, it was the Londoners' demand that stimulated the growth of brewing along the Thames. Some locally produced barley was sold already threshed and some was turned into malt by allowing the grain to sprout and then dry in a kiln. (A kiln was often shared by neighbours.) Strode produced a surplus of barley and prepared it for market in both ways. One Saturday, in September 1699, his man, Richard, took the malt to the maltman who ground three bushels. Strode spent the following Monday evening brewing. On another occasion, Palmer, the maltman from Staines, called on Strode to buy whatever barley he had already thrashed. The negotiations about the price took some time, so Strode was later than usual to his bed. A month later, in February 1700, when Strode was in London, he took a sample of Palmer's malt, produced from his own barley, to a London brewer. It would appear to be the opening approach to the sale of a larger quantity.

After barley, the other main cash crop was wheat. The surpluses of Staines and Egham would eventually have sold in the Brentford market. Although the largest corn market in the South-East was at Farnham and its hinterland, together with Essex, supplied most of London's corn, the produce of the Thames Valley ran a close second to these two centres. Upstream, Henley was becoming an important market. It had the great advantage of river transport that cost one-quarter of the price of transport by land. In the last decade of the 17th century average prices for all grains in the Home Counties were higher by as much as 25 per cent than prices for the South of England. Similarly, prices for hay, oats and pulses were over two-thirds higher than those obtaining in Cambridgeshire. As if in response to this agricultural boom, new fairs and markets were established. Chertsey had a new market in 1599, Staines gained a second fair, Windsor had three and Chertsey had four fairs.

Strode's diary gives some insight into the diet provided in a well-to-do household influenced by the sophistication of London.

55   The *Swan Inn* at the Hythe where Strode's goods from London were landed and where much of Staines'
trading took place. In 1678, it was the scene of the murder of one bargeman by another. The old wooden bridge
reached the bank just left of the building.

56   The *King's Head Inn* and part of Egham High Street looking west, 1822. The inn was used for vestry meetings and for the deliberations of the jury of the manorial court. Watercolour by John Hassell (1767-1825) who was a distinguished Surrey topographer.

There was a great deal of conviviality and entertaining among the gentry of the neighbourhood. One morning Strode's friend, Captain Castle (who farmed on Castle Hill, Engelfield Green), dropped in to borrow a flail and stayed to drink some of Strode's excellent claret and smoke a pipe. When a hamper of luxuries was brought up from the boat, Strode was very generous in sharing them with his friend: a dozen bottles of wine, six lemons, a gross of pipes, six pounds of tobacco and a wax candle. The grateful recipients invited Strode and his sister for a light supper, which consisted of 'pidgin pie, sturgeon, codlings and cream' washed down by two bottles of wine.

In February, the way to the Hythe, where the boats brought their cargo ashore, was too bad to take a cart down; so the hamper had to be left and only one special luxury, a jar of olives, was brought home. The consignment from London often contained

fish. In November there were a few bushels of oysters and soles. Fish was also provided locally. Strode had a cousin, Richard Terry, who was a fisherman and supplied perch, pike, salmon and tench from the Thames. He brought a five-pound salmon to Grovesend, for which Strode paid him 5s. 8d. (Henry VIII paid 20s. for one from the river at Staines in 1530.) On one family occasion, Strode provided a dinner of flounders and eels.

Local fare included beef and lamb and game such as hare and poultry (geese and capons). Usually when the diary gives details of a meal there are also vegetables – cabbage, parsnips and 'sallet' – to accompany the meat and fish. Sherry and wine, in particular claret, came in casks by river and was bottled at the house. There was fruit in plenty and Strode grew his own grapes.

The labour involved in producing the farm's income was intensive and unrelenting. The farm workers had a six-day week and did long hours when there was daylight to complete tasks against a change in the weather. Ploughing one and a half acres was reckoned as a day's work in the fine days of August. Late in October it took three men six days to plough and sow the six acres at Bellfields. Earlier, this ground had been spread with dung, much of it carried up hill from Egham – a task that took all of 10 days. On Cooper's Hill, Strode had land known as the Coppice that he had prepared for cultivation by having fresh soil carried there to improve and level the site. The normal day's work for two men was carrying and spreading five cartloads. Strode calculated that 121 loads of earth had been moved up to the Coppice, an area of four acres. The diary entry for Friday 8 September gives an

idea of the long hours and hard work. 'Our Folkes were at work betimes of carrying more Earth because it was Staynes Fair day. the Horses were brought by Anthony by two a Clock in the Morning. they carried their stint five loads ... all our Folkes went to Staines.'

Good preparation of the ground required a process called 'stirring' for both winter-sown wheat or rye or spring-sown barley. This was cross-ploughing the land that had already been turned over and it preceded harrowing. The aim was to break down larger clods of earth until a fine tilth, fit for sowing, was achieved. Often the land was too wet in early spring to respond to the treatment – indeed, there were days when it was impossible to get the horses out – and

57 Staines Moor looking towards the town.

then most farm jobs had to wait until the ground dried out. During February and March, Strode had his men ditching and trenching, the latter work at the Coppice to improve the drainage. These were the days before agricultural drains came into production. Little had changed since Leland twice crossed the district in 1538 and 1542 and commented on the 'low pasture' where 'at rages of rayne by rising of the river much over flowers'.

The richest land in both parishes was, nevertheless, the meadowland by the Thames. It was probably worth more than double the value of the arable. All farmers and cottagers kept animals, mainly cattle and pigs, though there were some sheep that were kept on the slopes of Cooper's Hill in Egham. The tradition of large tracts of grazing land and even of meadow remaining as common land continued in Staines and to a lesser extent in Egham. These were the so-called Lammas lands, named after the feast day celebrating the first fruits of harvest in early August. By then, hay had been taken by farmers who had the right to do so by manorial custom and the Lammas lands were open generally as commons for the grazing of animals until March. Staines Moor (now confined on the west by the M25 motorway and on the east by the King George VI Reservoir) remains as common land. It was associated with the sub-manor of Yeoveney and was traditionally used by the Abbot of Westminster as grazing for the whole manor. These customary grazing rights, known locally in both Staines and Egham as farrens, survived.

In Staines 'moor masters' were employed to control the grazing and look after the beasts. The office continues to the present day and its holders represent the rights of the commoners. In Egham there had also been ancient rights of grazing called 'agistment'. They had been the cause of much anger and conflict on the eve of the Civil War and did not survive the Restoration. However, though much more restricted than in Staines, Lammas grazing rights continued on Runnymede although, by the 1790s, according to Frederic Turner, there were only 10 owners of this rich meadowland. One of these was the successor to the Strode holding, the young architect John Vardy, assistant to William Kent in landscaping the Great Park for the Duke of Cumberland.

Chapter Seven

RESTORATION AND DISSENT

The calm surface of daily life at the end of the 17th century, as depicted by Henry Strode's diary, concealed the aftermath of the civil and religious conflict half a century earlier. Strode himself was a product of the religious ferment that reached its climax in the 1650s. Like very many of his contemporaries he was a serious student of theology. He wrote down his ideas on the fundamentals of his faith and his diary bears witness to the devotions that he referred to as his morning and evening exercises and his regular midnight 'soliloquy'. The latter was the hour he spent usually between midnight and 1 a.m. speaking to God on some predetermined topic. One theme to which he kept returning was the subject of Grace: the means by which the believer comes to repentance and, with God's help, struggles away from his unregenerate life towards a life guided by the Holy Spirit. With simple frankness, Strode finds himself constantly backsliding, in particular because of his loose tongue and his tendency to join in the local gossip and to enjoy what he called 'frothy conversation'.

The rigorous devotional life that Strode aimed at following was often referred to as 'closet piety'. The believer attempted to find 'hours of retirement that he might maintain his converse with God'. It was characteristic of many who had found the teaching, preaching and example of the established Church inadequate. They had therefore turned to ministers who had been allowed greater freedom of worship by Cromwell than had ever previously existed. When the monarchy was restored in 1660, these religious leaders and their congregations were required to conform to the national Church. A new prayer book, issued in 1662, imposed a single form of service and the accompanying Act of Uniformity required an oath of loyalty that many ministers could not, in conscience, take. In different ways, Staines and Egham experienced the consequences of this imposition of uniformity and intolerance. Both had ministers of a Presbyterian persuasion in 1660. Gabriel Price in Staines had been the longest serving of several ministers who had been welcomed by the majority to lead the community in the place of the pluralist parson, Dr Some. Since Price was, therefore, an 'intruder', no time was lost in evicting him and replacing him with a Crown appointee. The parish clerk recorded the resumption of the old norms of parish life in the register: 'After the blessed Restoration of King Charles, being presented to the vicarage by the king, Matthew Day names Thomas Skeet clerk and registrar.'

The loyalties of the people of Staines were divided. Mostly they kept quiet and accepted the status quo. Serious injustices, such as the billeting of troops, roused

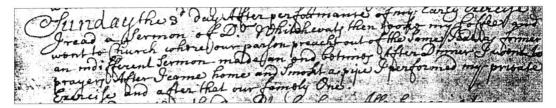

58 Henry Strode's diary, 1699, where he recorded his daily religious 'exercise' and the topic of his nightly 'soliloquy' with God. Such deeply felt personal devotion was characteristic of many contemporary dissenters and non-conformists. However, it did not prevent Strode commenting critically on the parson's sermons.

indignant protest. The parish clerk had indicated his disapproval of the actions of pro-Parliament churchwardens at the beginning of the Civil War and there is one glimpse of Royalist loyalty during the Protectorate, probably the result of an inebriated evening at an inn. Four men from Staines appeared before the magistrate at Brentford in August 1656 charged with drinking the health of King Charles and the Duke of York. One, Thomas Highho, a musician, was bound in recognisance for £40, while the others, Thomas West, gentleman, John Barrett, cook and Daniel Gylles, were bound for £20 each. These were surely meant as deterrent sentences. (Thomas West resumed public office in 1660 as one of the overseers of the poor rate.)

Even more crippling was the condition of Gabriel Price, evicted from his house, deprived of his income and subsequently threatened by restrictive legislation that carried heavy punishment. The new Royalist Parliament was much more intolerant than the King's inclination towards ex-Presbyterian ministers and others who dissented from the national Church. Price probably remained in the area and, if the later experience of William Reyner, the Egham minister, is a guide, members of his former congregation would have supported him. In February 1661, Reyner conducted the burial service of Gabriel's wife, Ann. The doubly deprived minister had a young family to support.

The Act of Uniformity made it impossible for Reyner to conform and take the oath of allegiance. He would have had to deny his past ministry, repudiate his oath to the Solemn League and Covenant, made with the Scots in 1643, and he would have been required to accept doctrines on baptism and Church ceremonies that he had hitherto rejected. On 24 August 1662, St Bartholomew's Day, Reyner, his assistant Richard Wavell and his two parson sons, Samuel and Daniel, all lost their livings and would have been destitute without the continued support of their parishioners. William Reyner continued living in Egham, was paid privately by his supporters and, according to his contemporary biographer, Edward Calamy (another evicted minister), 'preached as far as his strength allowed him and was never disturbed by the authorities'. From the Egham parish register, we also know that he continued to officiate at the parish church over burials of members of his family and others. In January 1676 he buried his little granddaughter, Mary. It would seem that Reyner acted much as Richard Baxter, a leading apologist for Nonconformity, did in Acton. In his autobiography Baxter wrote that sometimes he 'repeated the parson's sermon and sometimes taught such as came to my house between the sermons'. In 1676, according to the Compton Census, there were three Nonconformist families in Egham. A visitation return provided by

59 Churchwardens' accounts in the 1660s took care to record the costs of the twice-yearly visitation (inspection) by the Archdeacon of London. Normally the event was the clerk's journey to the archdeacon to give a report. Communion, taken twice and, later, four times a year was sufficiently rare to merit claret wine.

the Egham vicar, Thomas Wrightson, in 1725, reported that 'we have no meeting [of dissenters] of any kind. Not above five or six small families of Presbyterians, two of Quakers.'

In Staines there was a different story. From Henry Strode's diary for November 1699, we learn that one of his travelling companions in the London coach was the 'Presbyterian parson' of Staines. Three months earlier 'one that stood candidate for the Non-Conformists place at Staines' joined Strode's coach bound for London. Were they one and the same person? The

Presbyterian community in Staines seems to have grown quite strongly after 1662. A licence was granted under the Indulgence issued in 1672 for the members to meet for worship at the house of John James. He was the former rector of Ilsley, Berkshire, whence he had been evicted in 1662. He had a reputation as a good preacher and he was one of the teachers in a conventicle based on Wraysbury and Colnbrook, chosen as an area that avoided persecution under the 1665 Five-Mile Act. (This forbade evicted ministers from travelling within five miles of their former parish or any corporate town.) Brentford, having no corporate status, was, for a time, a popular centre for Nonconformity. In the Compton Census, Staines returned 28 Nonconformist families compared with three in Egham. When the Toleration Act, 1689, allowed public worship by Nonconformists and dissenters, 10 places in Middlesex had one or more churches. One of these was in Staines. The minister at that time was Robert Chantry, representing a second generation of Nonconformist ministers: his father had been evicted from his parsonage in 1662.

The rise of Quakers in and around Staines dates from the same period as that of the Presbyterians and for the same or similar reasons. Quaker meetings in Kingston (1654 or 1656) and Uxbridge (1658 or earlier) were the first in the area. The political vacuum in the 1650s, when there was no monarchy and no House of Lords, provided opportunities to challenge the monopoly of the national Church. Following a policy reminiscent of Mao's 'Let a hundred flowers bloom', Cromwell did little to crush the spread of alternative forms of Christian worship and associated experiments in seeking a more equable social order. Social, religious and political alternatives fed on each other and came to be regarded as threats to the body politic, to property and the moral law. Among the most extreme groups were Quakers and Ranters, frequently and wrongly confused but regarded with fear. The Quakers rejected all hierarchy in Church and society, believing that the spirit should rule supreme. For all these reasons they were savagely treated, especially in the years after 1660.

Richard Ashfield is generally credited with being the first Quaker in Staines. He was a maltster and was probably quite wealthy. In 1669 he was listed as giving one of the largest donations, 15s., towards 'those going beyond the seas'. These were Quakers emigrating to escape the intolerance and persecution that many of them found too hard to bear. In 1671, when the first written evidence provides proof of the existence of the Staines meeting, Ashfield and John Northcutt (or Northcott) headed a subscription list with gifts of £1 10s. and £1 respectively. According to his wife's testimony Ashfield had already, in 1665, suffered a year's imprisonment for refusing to take an oath. The year is significant since it marked a time of rising persecution and the passing of the Conventicle Act, making the holding and attending of religious meetings an offence.

The Staines meeting, at first held monthly and then fortnightly, was soon included within the London meeting, along with meetings from Westminster, Southwark, Ratcliffe, Wheeler and Peele. All of these were within London. In addition there was included the meeting from Enfield and the West Middlesex group consisting of Colnbrook, Longford and Uxbridge. In 1675 Richard Ashfield signed as the representative of Staines on the London meeting, although subsequently his name was deleted.

In the index of the first Kingston Quakers (Ellis Hookes' MS) several names of Staines residents occur, including those of Richard Ashfield and Ann Cooms. Later, in 1680 and 1693, Ann Cooms and Thomas Ashfield respectively were witnesses to marriages. Richard's name does not appear in 1670 when several Kingston members were convicted under the Conventicle Act. It seems likely that he was already helping to establish a Quaker meeting in Staines. The one at Longford had been established in 1669, meeting in John Northcutt's house. The authorities evidently harassed it because money was collected in London and Ireland to give relief to its members. Both Ashfield and Ann Cooms appeared before the magistrates for breaking the Conventicle Act.

Northcutt and Ashfield were instrumental in providing a meeting house and a burial

60   Congregational church, 1837, destroyed in 1956 to widen the junction between Thames Street and the High Street. Michael Robbins called it 'a severe little classical building'. It had hat racks under the seats. It marked the continuation of a substantial body of dissent stretching from the 1650s. (Copyright of Surrey History Service.)

61 Church Street, Staines. Many of its 18th-century houses survive, several of them having been homes to members of the Ashby family.

ground for Longford. Northcutt bought land near the highroad at Longford, paying £17 for it, and London members subscribed towards the cost of the building. In 1676, Ashfield was arrested for Nonconformity and once again imprisoned in Newgate 'to the great Grief and Trouble of many honest People who wept when they took their leave of him'. Joseph Besse contains the tragic and touching account of Ashfield's imprisonment in a collection 'of the Suffering of the People Called Quakers' made in the 1750s. Patience Ashfield related her husband's suffering in the cold, damp and stinking prison that was Newgate. He was already, by the standards of the time, an old man at 65 when he was committed to gaol. He died the following year in October 1677 and was buried at Longford. The forebodings of his friends in Staines had proved well-founded.

Patience continued 'sted fast in the Faith [and] was enabled also to suffer for her Constancy in attending Meetings'. The 'Collected Sufferings' relates how Patience owed a fine of £10 for attending two meetings at Longford and 'for an unknown Preacher'. The account continues: 'William Field, Constable … demanded entrance … fetched an Iron Crow and attempted to break open the Street-door.' Having failed in this he found the back door weaker and made

his entry. In Patience's own words he made 'no demand of the Money nor letting me see the Warrants, presently fell upon my Goods, laying them in bundles to carry them away'. He claimed £20 and actually took away £26 or £28 worth of goods. Patience was undeterred by this persecution and blatant injustice. From 1685 her house was used by the Quakers of Staines for their fortnightly meeting, paying 40s. a year as rent. Younger than Richard by 15 years, she lived on into a more tolerant age and died in 1704 or 1708.

By this time the Staines Quakers were anxious for a proper meeting house, and this had been made legal by the Act of Toleration in 1689. John Tanner bequeathed £20 towards the cost in 1710 and this enabled the purchase of the freehold of an old barn for £33 from Thomas Berryman of Chertsey. The site was at the sign of the *Black Boy* in Blue Anchor Lane, which ran from the High Street down to the Thames and was subsequently known as Quaker Lane. Money for the building, amounting to £120, was raised locally and a further £70 was contributed by the London meeting.

Other Staines members shared Patience Ashfield's experience of persecution during the 1680s. To some extent this persecution was provoked, though never justified, by the

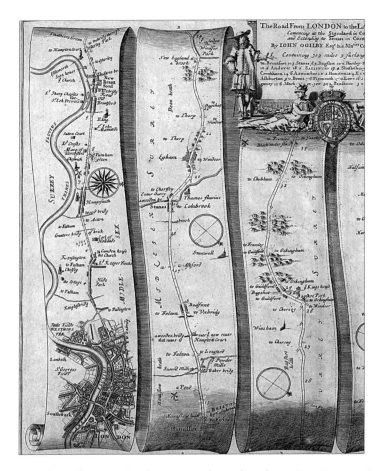

62 Ogilby's strip map for travellers, 1675, showing the route Egham and Staines folk would have taken to London. Some might have taken a boat from Brentford as Henry Strode did. Ogilby indicates that the bridge was a wooden one, repaired after the damage of the Civil War.

practice of some Quakers attending church services and interrupting the parson to dispute points of theology and ceremony. What appeared as extreme behaviour, showing no deference to people of higher social status and refusing to bow or remove their hats, was regarded as seriously as breaking the law by attending 'conventicles' and refusing to pay rates and tithes. They were feared because they were misunderstood. In his collection of material about the Quakers in Staines, Eric Butterfield relates an occasion in 1682 when a meeting in a barn was spied upon. The evidence survives as sworn testimonies and in the record of the Quarter Sessions. The informants claimed some 40 people were present (actually it was nearer 30), and

that Jeremy Frowsell preached. There is an interesting list of some of the company, which included several of the most prominent and respected members of the local community. They included John Cooper, a maltster, John Andrews, a mealman, Roger Lewis, a brewer (all three trades becoming important in Staines), John Estwick, a grocer, Simon Saunder, a fisherman and Henry Saunders from Egham, a constable and therefore a law enforcer.

The social composition of the Staines meeting contained many such middle-ranking, prosperous traders. Many were described as yeomen, a few as gentlemen and several families were represented who would have been regarded as public-spirited pillars of the community. These were the families whose members regularly served as churchwardens, overseers, constables and surveyors. Michael Dorsett, who had been churchwarden in 1680, was in court in 1690 for using his house as a 'Meeting House for dissenting Protestants'. Another member of the Dorsett family, Martha, was before the Bench in June 1682 for attending a Quaker meeting. Two groups consisting of six and 10 Quakers were charged in 1682 (a year when the Staines members appear to have been under close observation), but juries acquitted them. Perhaps their good names and reputations within the west Middlesex community had a bearing on the judgement of their peers.

The community was still quite small, its members well known to one another and strangers tended to be held in suspicion as most were travellers, vagrants, poor and homeless, and liable to become a charge on the rates. Staines was little more than a village. It probably had about 800 inhabitants by comparison with about 1,200 in Egham. Paterson's *Roads* described it as 'situated on a high road, principally composed of houses on each side forming one wide street'. The contrast in size between the two places would not have been immediately obvious since Staines was a compact settlement, while Egham was a large parish with dispersed communities.

The evidence for the size of the two populations is not simple to interpret and should, therefore, be treated as a rough guide. For Egham there is firstly the hearth tax return of 1662 based on hearths, both domestic and industrial, so ovens, forges and kilns were included. However, there were generally many exemptions including most dwellings with only one or two hearths. Egham appears to have had few exemptions and a total of 745 taxable hearths. These

included some buildings with as many as 14 hearths. Rather more helpful in making a calculation of the total population is the Compton Census. In 1676 Bishop Compton of London was responsible for a national survey of parishes. This asked for the number of communicants, Nonconformists and Papists. Egham's return was 800, three and four respectively. It is probable that the latter two figures represent families rather than individuals. The estimated population of 1,200 is reached by adding children under 16 who, as non-communicants, were excluded from the census.

The comparable hearth tax figures for Staines are 210 taxable hearths and five properties with more than 10 hearths. The Compton Census produced a return of 542 communicants, 2 Papists and 28 Nonconformists. These figures, adjusted to allow for the population under 16 years of age, produce a population of 760, just about two-thirds that of Egham.

Family names recur frequently in the records as one generation after another held public office and inherited copyhold land. The names Bartholomew, Fields, Wickes (or Weeks) and Saunders spread not only in both parishes of Staines and Egham but also across two to three centuries. Fortunes changed, of course. In the 1640s George Styles was receiving parish relief to support his family when illness struck down the breadwinner; yet in the 1750s and 1760s Styles served as overseer of the poor. In the 16th century the Standens aspired to the social status of gentlemen, one of them becoming vicar of Egham. By the late 17th century, Billy Standen was Henry Strode's pensioner and part-time farm worker.

A clutch of new families came into parish offices after the eviction of the minister, Gabriel Price, probably and inevitably following the swing of political fortunes.

63 St Mary's Church from the river. (Copyright of Surrey History Service.)

Even so, the divisions, such as they were in the 1640s and 1650s, did not form deep or permanent rifts and there were some families who found it possible to continue holding office at intervals throughout the mid-century upheavals. Richard Lidgold was churchwarden in 1632, a Lidgold was responsible for raising the rate to support injured soldiers in the Marshalsea hospital in 1653 and 1654 and paid his church rate on the parsonage. John Lidgold was active in the affairs of the parish vestry in 1715. From the mid-17th to the late 18th centuries the Mackason (or Mackeson) family improved their fortunes, building up substantial land holdings in Staines, Egham and further afield. Two Andrews, senior and junior, were churchwardens, followed later by John and Richard being active on the Staines vestry.

Those who undertook the duty of churchwarden needed to be financially secure. On many occasions the vestry expenditure exceeded the income from church rates. The deficit was borne by the churchwardens and they had to wait, sometimes for more than a year, before they were reimbursed by their successors. Expenditure was variable and unpredictable, collection unreliable and the account book not always written up.

Frequently it was completed a year or more later when new officers determined to be more efficient than their predecessors. In 1698, Mr Bonsey appeared as a new-broom churchwarden, not only taking charge of rate collection, but also keeping the account book. That year income amounted to £36 17s. 8d., rose two years later to £47 9s. 3d. and in 1704 £94 was the total.

At the turn of the century the regular payments included minor repairs to the church, new seats in some pews, prayer books, communion wine (always claret), expenses for the visitation – the archdeacon's inspection – usually in the form of the clerk's expenses in travelling to London to make the parish's report and washing the surplices. Some poor relief was paid mainly to help penniless travellers on their way so that they would not become a heavier charge on the rates and to parish orphans to set them up in apprenticeships. In practice these children could look forward to little more than farm labouring for the boys and household service for the girls. One chilling payment entered in the 1696 churchwardens' accounts was for the purchase of a lock and chain for Mad Mary.

Chapter Eight

INNS, ROADS AND MEALMEN

In January 1695, inn holders and churchwardens John Beauchamp and William Connop affirmed before the Brentford magistrates that they and 10 other inn holders in Staines were owed a total of £24 13s. 2d. for providing quarters for Captain Coward's company of Dragoons. A year earlier William Cook of the *Red Lion* and John Love of the *Angel* made a similar claim on behalf of the Staines inn holders for £119 unpaid by Captain Fletcher's troops of horse. Although obtaining payment remained almost as difficult as during the Civil War, some progress had been made. There was more regulation with an agreed list of inn holders liable to provide quarter and a reasonable rate of payment settled at the Quarter Sessions.

The record of 1695 has other interest. Most of Staines' inns of the time are listed: *Anchor, Angel, Bear, Black Boy, Dog, Nag's Head, Red Lyon, Rose & Crown* and *White Horse*. (Three inn holders appear in the list without their inn's name attached, hence the discrepancy in numbers.) One leading inn missing from the list is the *Bush*, which, with the *Angel* and *Crown*, became the leading coaching inns. Some inns survived for centuries, others came and went. The *Blue Anchor* had 15th-century origins and stood opposite the *Bush*, which probably dated from the 16th century and had been known for certain since 1601. The *Angel,*

Cock, Hart, George and *Swan* were inns of 15th-century origin. The *Lion* was known in the 16th century and the *Bell* made its appearance in the 17th century. The number of inns demonstrates Staines' importance for travellers, situated as it was at the Thames crossing of the south-west highway. As the coach trade developed, the number of inns grew to as many as 20 during the 18th century, falling back to 11 or so in the 19th century (*V.C.H.* vol iii, Susan Reynolds). The *Bush* was demolished because of the new approach to the bridge (1832) and was rebuilt as the *Clarence*.

Egham was also well supplied with inns for the same reasons. Travellers to the south-west might well have pushed on beyond Staines and then preferred to spend the night in Egham in order to avoid the banditry of Bagshot Heath at dusk. The *Catherine Wheel* is the oldest recorded, leased to Richard Adamson by Chertsey Abbey in 1507 for 200 years. The Parliamentary Survey, 1650, gave it a value of £48 16s. 7½d., making it the most important of Egham's inns. It was a very large timber building, which included a hall and two parlours. There was stabling for 50 horses. In addition it had 'a shed for coal below stayers, a dozen good lodging chambers above, one granary and three hay-lofts, a thatched barn of three bays, an inward court and garden, neatly ordered, an orchard and a dung yard'. It stood on

64 The *White Lion Inn* dating from the 16th century and standing at a narrow part of the High Street towards its eastern end. It was demolished because it obstructed the flow of 20th-century traffic. (Copyright of Surrey History Service.)

the corner of the London road and Little Humber Lane (now Hummer Road) and in all covered about one acre.

The *King's Head*, which accommodated the vestry meeting and the Court Baron meetings in the late 17th century, was first mentioned in the parish register in 1616. It too had extensive stables, demolished in the mid-19th century according to the Egham historian Frederic Turner, but the inn's activities continued to be recalled by cottages at the rear known as 'Post Boys Row'. All have disappeared beneath the development of the Egham Precinct. The *King's Head* and the *Catherine Wheel* appear to have been in competition for the 'quality' trade. It is believed that it is one of the *Catherine Wheel*'s parlours that features in Thomas Rowlandson's watercolour (1784) *Breakfast at Egham*. John Taylor, the water-poet who undertook marathon journeys for subscribers, first mentioned the *Crown* in the 1630s. Turner suggests it probably dealt with the wagon trade. Nearby, towards the

western end of Egham, the *King's Arms* was mentioned in the Court rolls in 1690 and the *Running Horse,* later the *Eclipse,* in 1650.

As in Staines, inns came and went. A property originally owned by the vicar of Egham in the 16th century and the subject of several decades of legal dispute up to 1650 became the *Whyte Lyon* inn and in the early 18th century, when owned by the Bartholomew family, was often the venue of the vestry meeting. The *Red Lion* probably became an inn only in the 18th century when its proximity to the assembly rooms gave it importance. Blue Ball Lane survives but its inn has long gone. Other inns are known only through their tokens, used as copper coinage, until the 1670s. One such was the *Buchars Arms*. The riverside at the Hythe had the *Swan*, which was used by bargemen and river traders.

The inns provided welcome relief for travellers from the jolts, bumps, mud-splashes and shaking of the journey. There

From the Middlesex Sessions

18 January 1695
Certificate affirming monies unpaid for quarters for Captain
Coward's Company of Dragoons. Commanded by Colonel Leigh.

(signed)   John Beauchamp
            William Connop

		£	s	d
John Wells	White Horse	4	19	11
Francis Harman		0	14	8
William Saunders	Rose & Crown	0	14	8
James Acton	Black Boy	0	11	4
Thomas Bell	Bear	0	14	5
William Field	Anchor	0	13	4
Richard Fortune	Dog	0	13	4
John Beauchamp		3	19	7
James Langley	Nag's Head	1	9	11
John Love	Angel	3	2	11
William Connop		4	4	1
William Cooke	Red Lyon	2	15	0
		24	13	2

65 Claims submitted on the authority of the churchwardens for the costs incurred by inn holders who had to billet soldiers.

was overnight accommodation, a change of horses, food, drink, oats and straw, interchange with other coach services and such additional services as the post and delivery of messages. On his way home to Egham, Henry Strode remembered he had not tipped his nephew's servant. At Brentford, where the Egham coach stopped to allow passengers and horses refreshment, he was able to scribble a note and send a man off with the message. The bustle and activity of arrivals, changes and departures also provided a source of news, gossip and profit for the locality. Saddlery, for example, became a major trade in Egham in the 18th century.

The inns were of considerable economic value to their neighbourhoods, providing a major source of employment, much of it casual and seasonal, which matched usefully with farm work. The growth in the number of inns also represented the expansion of a national road network and transport of goods by road. As the economy grew in the

17th century, so road transport responded. It had some key advantages over water transport, which, although essential for heavy and bulky goods, could also be very slow and, of course, had limited geographical scope. In 1637, pack-horse trains were run by approximately 200 carrier services. These were soon supplemented by wagon services and by the early 18th century the main carrier and coach networks had become integrated by cross-country services. The inns were at these important points of intersection.

Often the inn holders were the entrepreneurial pivot, owning or sharing ownership in one or more carrier routes, providing horses and distributing parcels, post and newspapers locally. Inn holders were, therefore, often men of substance. Connop, Beauchamp and Iliff served as churchwardens in Staines, Cotterell and Bartholomew were counterparts and contemporaries in Egham. Their names appear frequently in land transactions, taking up leases, providing a mortgage and generally building up a diverse and thriving business.

There was, however, a major problem for all whose business depended on the roads and that was their deteriorating condition as traffic increased. The nearer to London, the worse they were. It is true that many travellers' tales exaggerated the difficulties and discomforts but it is indisputable that, as the bulk trade in wagons increased, conditions worsened in the last decades of the 17th century. The wheels of the wagons wore down the surface into even deeper ruts, repairs that were the parish's responsibility were inadequate and the practice of damping down the surface to reduce dust in summer caused the accumulation of deep mud in winter.

Staines was in the heartland of the worst conditions. The problem was a long-standing one. Henry VII gave £2,000 for the repair of

66   The *Bush Inn* and the approach to the old bridge, 1828. This extensive old building with its pleasure gardens, ornamental shrubs, herbaceous border, stables and separate taproom was compulsorily purchased to allow for a new approach to the 1832 Rennie bridge. (Copyright of Surrey History Service.)

roads from Windsor to Staines and onward to Southwark via Richmond and then on to Canterbury. The road was to be wide enough for two carts to pass; it was to be ditched and the surface raised and gravelled to ensure it did not sink into a morass of mud in winter. The king's gift did not ease the problem of the local roads for long. Complaints multiplied as more traffic came in and out of London. Writing in the early 18th century, Defoe commented:

> … the whole kingdom as well as the people, as the land and even the sea in every part of it, are employ'd to furnish something and I may add the best of everything to supply the city of London with provisions.

Defoe added that the traffic in goods was not all one-way into London. The capital's population grew from 200,000 in 1600 to 575,000 in 1700. Its food needs almost doubled while the country's output as a whole doubled during the 18th century. Little wonder that the roads crumbled. Brentford was renowned for its muddy approaches.

The Uxbridge road had only one passable track and was usually clogged with carts and wagons. From Hounslow both the Bath and the south-west roads were equally bad. It is not hard, therefore, to imagine the conditions exacerbated by Thames floods around Staines in the winter. According to a contemporary, 'there is no riding even in boots and a horseman's coat during half the year!'

One solution that was sought as early as 1663 was the setting up of trusts, by private Acts of Parliament, to repair existing roads and then maintain them from the income of tolls on wagons, horses and coaches. It is not surprising that the majority of these early Turnpike Trusts were in Middlesex. The first to have an impact on Staines was the Brentford trust, set up at the second attempt in 1717. It was responsible for road improvements from Kensington to Cranford Bridge over the River Brent. Its extension, in 1727, was along the route of the Bath or Great West Road to Maidenhead Bridge.

This was followed closely by an Act setting up a trust for the road from Hounslow through Staines to Bagshot.

Local people led the demand for these improvements. The *House of Commons Journal* records that petitions were presented to Parliament in 1714 and these provide the evidence of public concern at road conditions.

> Deputy Lieutenants, JPs, Gentlemen and others living in or near the road from Kensington to Colnebrook and Staines [protested that] by reason of the many and heavy Carriages frequenting the said Roads, the same are becoming so very ruinous, that it is a danger to Her Majesty and all attending her to travel that way; and the Inhabitants thereof have been at great Expence in repairing the same, yet continue so bad that it cannot by the Laws now in Force be effectually mended with an Act of Parliament: Gravel and other Materials not being to be had but at a great Distance.

Petitioners included key road users; graziers, farmers, gardeners, higglers, carriers, stage-coachmen and waggoners. Together they represent a broad section of Staines society and indicate that the town's economy had become more entrepreneurial, more dependent on trade and far from self-sufficient. Improvements to other roads around Staines came much later. The routes north to Stanwell and Uxbridge and south to Laleham long remained mere lanes and not subject to the heavy traffic of the London-bound routes. It was not until 1773 that the establishment of a Turnpike Trust improved another important route, the one to Kingston. Badly as it was needed, the Staines vestry was reluctant to contribute. In 1776 the vestry meeting declared it would take responsibility for repairs only as far as the turnpike gate, the point at which tolls for the journey were taken.

The area remained prosperous. The influence of the London market kept up prices of both agricultural and horticultural produce while wage rates could be from one-third to one-half as high again as those around Oxford. Milling was an enterprise that provided several leading families in Staines with a good income. Flour from wheat and rye, meal from oats and malt from barley were their products. Along the Thames, milling and brewing became important industries and provided the basis for the great 19th-century breweries. Hops were already a widely planted crop in the 17th century – there was, for example, a hop ground in Laleham – and oast houses for drying hops and malt became a long-

67 The *Catherine Wheel Inn*, Egham, traditionally provided for the quality trade, along with the *King's Head* and, like the *Bush* and the *White Lion*, had medieval origins.

68 *Breakfast at Egham*,
watercolour by Thomas
Rowlandson, 1784, is believed
to depict the parlour of the
Catherine Wheel.

enduring feature of the townscapes of both Staines and Egham.

Two of Staines' mills have a long history. Hale Mill on the River Colne was mentioned in 1353 and probably dates from the 13th century. It is likely that it took its name from a tenant of Westminster Abbey called John de la Hale. The New Mill, mentioned in 1388, probably became a fulling mill in the 15th century and was situated near Moor Bridge over the western arm of the Wyrardisbury River (a little to the east of the Old Staines West railway station). It may have replaced the mill at Yeoveney to the north. Pound Mill came later. It was near the New mill and became part of the holding of the Finch family. Its stream was for some time known as Finch's (or Fisher's) Allowance.

The leading miller in the 17th century appears to have been Henry Palmer, followed by his son, Simon. Henry probably began in the trade in the late 1640s, just as the civil war was ending. It was not a propitious time with Staines' trade hindered by the destruction of the bridge and by the large companies of soldiers billeted in and around the town. One member of the family was, for a time, in receipt of poor relief in the form of three pairs of shoes, while Henry himself paid only 8d. in rates on what must

have been a very modest property. Edward Palmer became churchwarden, chosen by the newly restored vicar in 1660 and thereafter regularly attended vestry meetings. This alone would have made him an important and influential member of the community. There were two other Palmer households, one headed by Joseph and Margaret, another by John and Elizabeth. The latter had a shop and a large family but neither couple appeared to be particularly prosperous. On the other hand Henry Palmer's son, Simon, prospered in milling, chiefly as a maltster, working Pound Mill and probably holding a lease on the mill upstream at Hythe End. In 1715 he was paying 17s. in rates for his house, Thorpes, and 15s. for the Pound mill. He was, therefore, among the most prosperous townspeople with a business that had expanded sufficiently for Henry Strode to take note and help him to find custom in London.

By 1740, the milling business had been relinquished by the Palmer family and from 1742 John Finch secured leases on two former Palmer mills, Hale and Pound, together with a house, a meadow known as Mill Mead, a barn and other land. John and his family were Quakers and became increasingly prosperous during the next 30 years. The family moved into the Staines area: the name does not appear earlier in the registers nor in the hearth tax returns for 1662, but John Finch married Dorian Tanner in Staines in 1728.

The Palmers, nevertheless, remained a family of some substance with property in Staines to which they kept adding. During the 1750s William Palmer served a term as churchwarden and leased the vicarage land. His son, also William, was one of only 32 property owners assessed for land tax in 1767. He also took over the lease on Herring's land, which consisted of more than 100 acres in the Staines open field, near the river in Laleham, in the east end near the junction of the Kingston and London roads and at the *Crooked Billet*. (It had been purchased by a London merchant, Henry Herring, as part of the endowment of Strode's charity set up in Egham by 1707 under the will of Henry Strode, 1704.) Edward Palmer had acquired land in Egham on Callow Hill, while Simon's property exceeded the value of the two mills.

The Finch family dominated milling for another 30 years until they sold their leases to another newcomer to the area, also a Quaker. This man was Thomas Ashby whose family was predominant in Staines in the 19th century. Thomas had learned the milling trade in Maidenhead, married in Laleham and came to Staines within the year in 1758, when he first appeared in the records paying rates on a very modest house. By 1779 he had prospered sufficiently to take over the Finch empire. He secured the leases of the mill at Hythe End and at Wraysbury and purchased for £500 a large house, Corner End, from Thomas Finch together with 33 acres in Queen's Mead. He had already acquired Thorpe Mill and

69 Floods in Kingston Road, Staines, in 1947, the worst since 1894. They are a reminder of conditions which made travelling a miserable affair before flood control on the Thames, and surfaced roads.

70 Hops, which were widely cultivated around Staines and Egham to provide an essential ingredient of beer.

had a third share in a wharf and another property near Staines bridge. Eric Butterfield, who has studied the Ashby family papers, suggests that an elder brother, Robert, who was already established in the milling trade at Uxbridge, may have helped with capital. Thomas's father died in 1781, leaving him a modest inheritance of £250. By this time, Thomas was able to boast that he could make 5s. profit on grinding a sack of flour. He could produce 100 a week and have £1,200 income a year.

In the years after 1779, Thomas Ashby began amassing land and property in Staines. He acquired much of the southern side of the High Street from the *White Lion* yard at its eastern end to the church and land between the church and the river. He leased land in the old manor of Yeoveney stretching west from the church to the County Ditch,

which included all the modern recreation ground. In 1801, he bought land and another mill in Wraysbury. A new venture in 1796 was the founding of a bank. Within ten years Ashby bought out its competitor, the Middlesex and Surrey Bank, owned jointly by John Coggan of Laleham and John Morris, another Quaker.

Ashby was equally ambitious and successful in public affairs. As early in his career as 1762, he was an overseer of the poor, in spite of being a Quaker and refusing, from 1761, to pay his tithe. His large family of nine children ensured that he established a dynasty and dominated the Staines Quaker meeting. Two sons, Thomas and William, became his business partners while a third, Robert, began a coal-barging business in 1790, eventually buying his own barges and wharf.

At mid-century, Staines was still a close-knit, compact community, its built-up area clustering tightly along the High Street from the Kingston Road junction to the bridge. One new development that is clear on the 1768 Rocque map is the string of properties on either side of the curve of Church Street, connecting the market place and the church. No longer was the church isolated on its little hill. Several of these houses survive to make the area the only fragment of townscape to give an impression of the old town before its heart was ripped out in the 1960s and 1970s.

In 1750 a new broom was at work bringing order and a new level of consistency to the town's affairs. The books of the churchwardens and overseers begin to be kept neatly and clearly, whereas in the past several years at a time might be omitted and then partially written up from memory. The new clerk, Ezra Cottrell, kept the books with obvious pride in his work. He signed in a large, beautifully formed hand and wrote a preface in the new accounts book. 'This book', he announced, 'cost a five shilling journey by Horse and Shaies' to London. At the beginning he drew up a table for the church rate, showing the yield from a halfpenny in the pound up to 2s. in the pound. The range was £7 1s. 6d. to £340, a level that was never even approached. In the earlier entries he helpfully put the rateable value of each property in the left-hand margin so it is possible to gain some idea of people's relative wealth. Four pence in the pound was set for many years; then it dropped to 2½d. in 1759, rising for a short period to 6d. in the 1760s.

Among the ratepayers, family names appear attesting to continuity of family and residence for generations. They include Saunders, one of whom was a nurseryman, Daubon (Henry supplied leather for the bell clappers) and Mackason, whose interests and land acquisitions had spread to Egham, where Andrew had recently purchased meadowland for fattening cattle. He was a butcher. There were notable newcomers as well, who were landowners although not always resident. They included the Earl of Harborough, Sir James Lowther and Daniel Pontifex, who paid one of the largest rates. In 1754 it amounted to one-eleventh of the total collected. Pontifex took his turn as churchwarden. Other familiar names continued to feature since plots of land were frequently identified by their owners or former owners' names: Lidgold's orchard; Mrs Love's orchard, Watt's cherry ground, Brown's piece, Pinnock's mead. On the river there were Stone's Ait, Limbrey's Ait, Watt's Ait and Savery's Weir.

Occasionally the vestry had to deal with the legal side of a personal tragedy. In 1759 Mr Neve's maid committed suicide by drowning herself in his pond. A coroner's jury of 24 was called, each being paid 4d. for their attendance at a house especially hired for the coroner's court. The vestry had to deal with a legal dispute that appears to have run on over more than a decade in the 1750s and 1760s, in which the right to the vicar's tithe was challenged. The clerk failed to make the details clear. However, on a more mundane level, he meticulously recorded the payments made for vermin caught by various parishioners. In one year £1 2s. 9d. was paid

71   Bridge over the Wyrardisbury River on Hale Street. The road to the left led towards Pound Mill, the site of Walton's linoleum works for a century from 1864.

out for 91 dozen sparrows; while stoats (13), weasels (23), hawks (three), hedgehogs (30), polecats and others merited 4d. each.

Each year there was a town celebration of the Gunpowder Plot and the church rate paid for the 'spraies' or branches used to build the bonfire. The town went 'A Prossessioning' in 1757, incurring 14s. chiefly for dinner, wine and beer. This may refer to the annual Rogationtide processing, beating the bounds of the parish to remind everyone of their town's territory. There was also a keen awareness of European events. The Duke of Cumberland, George II's son, was leading Hanoverian troops in the Rhineland, directing the attention of the French from England's new ally, Prussia. In

1757, when the King of Prussia, Frederick the Great, was winning spectacular, if costly, victories in Silesia, Staines celebrated his birthday 'at the request of several people'. Tantalisingly, there was no indication of who were these Prussophiles. There was a bonfire, a procession with garlands and the ringing of the recently restored church bells. The ringers were rewarded with the usual (and generous) dole of beer. There were more special ringing days, perhaps celebrating the news of military victories. Two guineas' payment for the ringers was quite exceptional. In 1759, the 'annus mirabilis' of English victories, the taking of Quebec and victory over the Austrians at Minden, were marked. The Staines ringers

73 Ashby's malt house and, behind, brewery tower, built in 1903 and still a dominant symbol of the town and the Ashby family.

74 Egham High Street, western end. The triple gabled building, right, was known as the Old Bank and became part of Thomas Ashby & Co. in 1866.

75 Churchwardens' accounts showing payments made for 'vermin' which included sparrows.

continued longer than usual for the taking of Lemburgh (Limburgh).

There seemed to be a prevailing mood of confidence and optimism, demonstrated in these celebrations of royal occasions, victories and traditional festivals. The church bells were mended and rehung, a new flagpole was purchased and the church surroundings were smartened with new railings, boundary posts and turf and gravel laid in the churchyard. George III's coronation in 1760 was duly rung in with 5s. of beer money, a bonfire and special prayers.

Chapter Nine

THE NEW BRIDGE

That crucial link, Staines bridge, seems always to have had a chequered history. For centuries it decayed while disputes raged about where responsibility for its upkeep and repair rested. The tolls were inadequate and the bridge had always been disadvantaged in having no chapel, which might have provided extra income from pious and thankful travellers. The damage caused by the Civil War took decades to repair adequately and the bridge was still only a wooden one in 1712. The last royal oak to be used for repair was in 1713. Both the bridge and the Egham causeway suffered flood damage, probably annually. A ferry operated to convey horses across where the towpath was not continuous and it came to be used for passengers. In 1732 the parish contributed 10s. towards the cost of ferrying people to church. Two years later an Act of Parliament 'for the most effectual and well-keeping' of the bridge and the Egham causeway marked the beginning of almost a century of attempts to provide a safe and serviceable bridge.

The 1734 Act stated the problem clearly. The bridge was 'in a ruinous and dangerous condition' and the causeway was 'in danger of being broken through by Floods'. The bridge master kept a ferry but 'at an exorbitant rate' and 'to the great inconvenience and oppression of all persons travelling that way'.

There was also criticism of the inadequacy of income for maintenance, amounting to no more than £40 per annum.

Toll-dodging had become an art; so had the response of the bridge masters. They used a log to block the navigation arch under the bridge. Nothing more happened for 40 years when a commission of 14 was set up, representing Surrey and Middlesex equally, to oversee a new bridge. One of the commissioners, Thomas Sandby, a member of the Duke of Cumberland's staff since 1743 and his deputy as Ranger of the Great Park at Windsor, was chosen to design the new bridge. Although trained in the military drawing office at the Tower of London, a founder member of the Royal Academy, its first Professor of Architecture and Architect of the King's Works, Sandby had a notoriously poor record as an engineer. His design of the dam to contain the pond head of Virginia Water had collapsed dramatically in 1768 and again in 1784. Sandby earned the soubriquet 'Tommy Sandbank'.

The model for the bridge was the one Sandby had designed to carry the new line of the south-west road over Virginia Water. It was steep and triple-arched. The design for Staines had a central arch of 60 feet flanked by two arches of 52 feet. In addition there were two narrow arches to take the towpaths. The bridge was constructed in four years by an Oxford firm (Townsend &

76 The construction of Sandby's stone bridge, 1791, with the central arch still supported by timbers. Behind is the old wooden bridge showing a coach going towards Egham. Engraving from a painting by J.M.W. Turner.

Weston) but within two years of its opening it had cracked and had to be closed. The architect, Sir John Soane, reporting on the accident, blamed not the design but poor workmanship. However, the problem was more serious: it was structural and could not be remedied because of the lack of depth in the riverbed for the piers.

A second attempt followed on quickly using newly fashionable cast-iron, which had proved a success at Coalbrookdale and was being considered as a replacement for London Bridge. The commissioners consulted George Rennie but the design was by James Wilson. To avoid what was believed to be the main problem with Sandby's bridge, a single arch of 181 feet with stone abutments was chosen. It cost £4,900 and was constructed between 1801 and 1803. Within two months, the iron cracked and the abutment on the Middlesex side was moved back several inches by the force exerted from the arch. Masonry from Sandby's bridge was sunk behind the abutment to act as a countervailing buttress.

It was a failure and the bridge itself was written off.

The commissioners and their advisers returned to cautious and old methods for the third attempt. It was made possible by an Act of Parliament (1804), which allowed the borrowing of £6,000 and the continuation of tolls as before: horses 1d. or 2d. if laden; boats 3d. or 4d. if laden. Staines and Egham inhabitants had free passage. The bridge was to be built of timber. Rennie was the consultant. He insisted on strengthening the structure against the volume and weight of traffic with cast-iron plates. Iron-clad piles, 48 in number, gave sturdy support. Completion was celebrated in less than two years with a dinner at the *Bush Inn* for the commissioners and Rennie. However, for all the care and caution, the bridge had two great disadvantages. Its navigation openings were too narrow and it was very costly to maintain. Rennie and later his sons made an annual inspection. By 1827 repairs were estimated at over £11,000, much more than the initial cost, and four-fifths of the structure needed replacing.

An Act of Parliament in June 1828 gave new commissioners power to borrow up to £60,000 against the dubious security of the tolls. John Rennie produced preliminary sketches for a bridge very similar to his beautiful and successful Waterloo Bridge (1817) and insisted, against the doubts and some resistance from the commissioners, that it be built of granite. It had three arches and a 36-foot wide roadway. Rennie insisted on another condition: that the site be moved upstream where the riverbed provided better foundations than the old site. The consequences of this were compulsory purchase, the demolition of property and new approach roads.

There was much to be done to achieve the land purchases necessary to connect the newly positioned bridge scheme to the town's main arteries, the High Street and Church Street, which crossed the River Colne and led to the newer development of gentlemen's houses approaching St Mary's Church. The old *Bush Inn* was most affected since its property was so extensive, running from the west side of the High Street at the approach to the old bridge, across the River Colne at its confluence with the Thames and west across the proposed approach to the new bridge as far as the new Bridge Street. The

77   The new Sandby bridge, 1799. The old bridge can be seen through the arches.

Bush had gardens, a lawn and meadow on its site in addition to stabling for 100 horses. It was a flourishing business. From 1825 to 1827 the out-going lessee had an income of £4,132 from the tavern side of the business and £7,348 from posting. In 1827, just ahead of negotiations about the new bridge, the new lessee, William Hills paid £205 in rent. He left in 1830 before compensation could be agreed. The bridge commissioners' offer had been £4,000 but the landlord wanted at least one-third more.

William Holgate, whose shop occupied another prime site where the second new road, Clarence Street, was planned to meet the junction of Church Street and High Street, was offered £1,000. He wanted £1,400 and eventually settled by splitting the difference. There were other problems, more human than legal. John Spencer, who kept marine stores on Church Street (affected by the plan to widen the street), 'keeps no books and his income', wrote the Clerk to the Commissioners, Randolph Horne, 'is difficult to estimate'. This must have been true of many shopkeepers. Another distressed occupant claimed, 'We have not at present a house to go to and there are nine of us in the family'. An under-tenant of the brewers, Ramsboton & Leigh, found himself temporarily on the wrong side of the law when his goods were seized in error.

The *Red Lion* was neighbour to the *Bush*, but smaller and in a less prominent, though still valuable, site at the approach to the bridge. Its landlord, William Dearle, wrote to the commissioners in 1828 that his 'mind His made up to take 4000£ and know less'. The figure was his opening offer. It was not accepted so he had recourse to the professional services of a surveyor and, although he resented the £60 fee, he succeeded in achieving a purchase price of

78   Mr and Mrs Thomas Sandby by Paul Sandby.

£3,900 and remaining a further two years in his property. Even more successful was Isaac Willoughby, round the corner in Church Street, who reckoned that his property was worth £500 even though burdened with repairs. He was offered £400 but stuck out and eventually won the day. His tenant was less fortunate. Poor Thomas Davis had nowhere to go. Where land alone was required there were fewer complications and, in some cases, no challenge to the commissioners' offers. The *Cock Yard* lost 11 perches (approximately 275 square yards) and received £50 compensation. Thomas Ashby, whose pasture the new Bridge Street crossed, was required for £150 to surrender the width of the road, calculated at 1 rod 4 perches.

Two more Acts of Parliament were required to achieve all these changes (1829 and 1831). The contractors were Joliffe & Banks. It was an unusual but very successful partnership headed by the Revd William Joliffe and Edward Banks, a navvy whom Joliffe had met working on the Surrey Iron Railway at Merstham. The final cost came to a little over the estimate at £42,000, of which the bridge itself cost £23,800, the approach roads £7,160 and the removal of the old bridge £11,500. It was a remarkable result, triumphantly celebrated on St George's Day, 1832. As a commissioner, the Duke of Clarence had laid the foundation stone on the Surrey side on 14 September 1829. Sir William Fremantle performed the task on the Middlesex bank. By the time of the bridge's completion, the Duke had succeeded his brother as King William IV and asked to perform the opening ceremony. The event was royally celebrated, probably as much in relief as in triumph that, at long last, Staines had a sound and graceful bridge.

According to *The Times*, the king looked 'as if he had recently experienced an attack of the gout as at first he walked rather lame and stooping'. At either end of the bridge were 'two superb triumphal arches decorated with laurel and profusely adorned with appropriate emblems'. After the ceremony came the celebratory meal at which 100 guests sat down in the new *Clarence Hotel*. It was 'dressed with laurel and evergreens and hung round with red striped bunting'. The band of the 9th Lancers entertained the diners.

Improvements had meanwhile been made to the towpath by constructing a continuous length on the Surrey side for one-third of a mile below the bridge to the 'shooting off' place. The barge trade flourished up to the mid-century. In 1849, Ashbys, William Holgate and James Smith operated weekly to Queenhithe in London, and it was estimated that seven barges a week were arriving in

79   Bridge Cottage, The Hythe, showing the remains of the southern abutment of the Sandby bridge.

80 Bridge designed by George Rennie to replace the disastrous iron structure (1803) which cracked soon after its opening. This bridge had iron-clad supports but the cost of maintenance led to its replacement in 1828-32.

Staines carrying over 400 tons of goods. Coal was a major commodity. The Corporation of the City of London had jurisdiction over the river and levied a tax on all coal and wine that was transported. Traditional cast-iron boundary markers were set up to remind traders of this fact. Originally the coal tax had been introduced to help pay the costs of rebuilding St Paul's after the Fire of London. It became increasingly valuable to defray the cost of improvements, street-widening and paving and later it paid off the city's debts. According to Maurice Bawtry, 257 such posts were recorded in Staines in 1887, counted for maintenance purposes. The city's activities were taken over in 1862 by the Metropolitan Board of Works, a distant forerunner of the Greater London Council, and proceeds from the coal tax eventually paid off the loan that had been raised to free the bridge from tolls. This was an event for celebration as *The Times* recorded two days later on 27 February 1871.

Another reminder was the London Stone, which was probably set in its modern site in 1620 and given a new pedestal in 1781. During the 19th century it became a tradition for the lord mayor to be rowed up to the boundary of the city's jurisdiction to claim the city's rights and to drink its health. Crowds used to gather because money was often distributed. These events tended to degenerate into 'buffoonery and mere jollification', the Thames historian Fred Thacker observed. The buffoonery probably referred to the undignified ceremony of the 'bumping', by the watermen, of any alderman who had not been made 'free of the waters'.

The new bridge was widely regarded as an aesthetic as well as an economic asset to the town. Hunt's *Directory* for 1846 comments on its 'exquisite design'. Contemporaries were observant of the enhancement of the approach from the west. In particular Clarence Street, which was entirely new, 'formed a graceful and respectable entrance into the town'. Demolition provided the opportunity for new and admired buildings 'in accord with the style and taste of the bridge'. The ancient *Bush Inn* was rebuilt as the *Bush & Clarence* and remained, like its predecessor, an important post house and hotel. Its proprietor, John Collins, boasted royal appointment. In 1835, Sir William Fremantle laid the foundation stone for a Bible Institute, used later as a depository for the British & Foreign Bible Society and supervised by the vicar, the Revd Robert Govett. There was an elegant institute for 'literary and scientific purposes', which also had a lecture room and a library with a reading room.

During the first half of the 19th century change was slow but certain. Population estimates became more reliable as the three early censuses provided overall figures. (The detail was not generally published until the 1841 census.) In 1801, the town's population was 1,750, and almost 2,500 in 1831. For that year Robson's *Directory* published an analysis of occupations. The gentry were listed as numbering 19, an increase of two households since 1798. Farmers numbered 10, employing 34 labourers; manufacturers 20, retailers or craftsmen 232, labourers 253 (non-agricultural) and 22 domestic workers. These figures suggest a swing away from dependence on farming or smallholding. They should, however, be read with caution since many retailers and craftsmen may have derived some income from farming, as had been traditional.

The trades and crafts indicate a fairly self-sufficient community. In 1798, there was a carpenter, cabinet-maker, coach-maker,

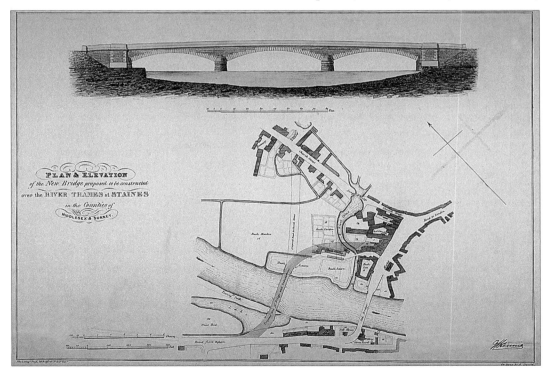

81   The fourth and successful design by John Rennie for Staines' new bridge, 1828. It was to be built of stone on a new site upstream away from the current produced by the confluence of the River Colne with the Thames. The plan shows the first idea of a new road to the bridge.

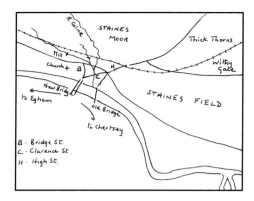

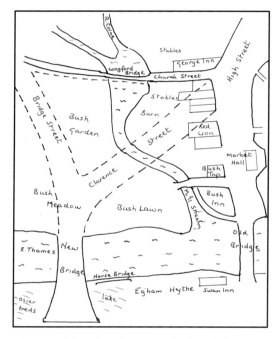

82 Sketch based on the surveyor's plan of the new bridge and projected approach roads. It also indicates where compulsory purchase of property was needed.

cooper, bricklayer, glazier-plumber, smith, tin-man and brazier, basket-maker, net-maker and harness-maker. Amongst the retailers were six grocers, two butchers, a baker and a range of specialists providing clothing and fashion: breeches-maker, collar-maker, linen draper, hatter, hairdresser-parfumier, shoemaker and tailor. Victuallers selling food and drink were the innkeepers

but there were also three shopkeepers plying a trade that probably consisted mainly of beer and spirits.

There was one general clothes shop and a Staffordshire-ware shop providing affordable ironstone ware and more expensive porcelain for the table, replacing old-fashioned pewter and wood. The number of grocers had increased to 12, including a few specialising in bacon, cheese and sundries. By the 1830s, Staines had three tea merchants, an indication that a once-expensive luxury had become more attainable as taxes were lowered. Two confectioners, six bakers, two watch and clockmakers, a haberdasher, three milliners, a dressmaker, two bookseller-stationers and two saddlers suggest a modest growth in population and in affluence. Some retailers continued to combine a retail outlet with a wholesale business, for example Joseph Tilly, who had a baker's shop in the High Street and was also a wholesale supplier of flour.

The town's trade was largely internal and local although, from the 1820s, there were at least three barge owners at any one time taking corn and other heavy goods to London and bringing coal upstream to Staines wharf. Until the arrival of the railway in 1848, the coach and carrier trade, using the Great West Road, meant that the town 'enjoyed for a number of years the fruits of an immense throughfare'. There were eight coaches for London and one from Windsor daily that changed horses at Staines, as well as others which stopped there. The *Bush & Clarence* and the *Angel & Crown* were the main posting houses. By 1846, Loft's omnibus left at 7 a.m. and returned at 7.30 p.m.

The long-established trades of milling and brewing became central to the town's prosperity. At the beginning of the 19th century, the Ashby family was the main

83 Coal tax post near Staines Bridge. A reminder of the City of London's right to impose taxes on the transport of coal and wine.

employer. The Finch family diversified and added mustard-making to their flour-milling business. William Murrell milled flour at the Hale Mill and William Harris with sons Thomas and John were brewers. These trades provided steady employment to a large number of families and contributed principally to the town's economic stability during the 1830s and 1840s, when the Midlands, the West Country and North were suffering extremes of poverty accompanied by social and political unrest. It was the era of Chartist activity. By contrast, Staines had a prosperous aspect, in part brought about by the opportunity given by the bridge's construction to erect some fine public buildings. These were matched by a scattering of new houses in the town and its immediate neighbourhood for the gentry, many of them newcomers to the area.

The most valued and spectacular modern facility was the provision of gas, introduced in 1833 from gas works on the Surrey side of the Thames by the Egham causeway. For an age used to true darkness at night, the sight of lights on the bridge reflecting in the water and visible from Egham hill two miles away was 'surprisingly beautiful'. The author of

Pigot's *Directory* for 1834 was quite carried away. 'It is another of those English displays which surpasses in its reality of brilliancy and enchantment all that the tales of Arabia and Persia have ever portrayed.' Altogether the accumulative effect of the new public buildings, 'several new commodious, tasteful houses', the rebuilt parish church and a new brewery was an 'exhibition of freshness and respectability that contrasts most agreeably of [*sic*] Hounslow and Brentford'. The other side of this picture is a river so polluted that the salmon disappeared after 1840.

Although Staines had no endowments, it achieved a good provision of schools. Early in the 19th century these were mainly private ones: the vicar, Mr Govett, ran a boarding school for gentlemen at the vicarage, while a ladies' boarding school existed in the High Street in 1798 and may have been the same institution run in the 1840s by the Misses Ollive and Billingshurst. Day schools providing basic literacy and numeracy together with the elements of Christian faith and morals were supported voluntarily and run by two nationwide religious societies. The National schools were affiliated to the Church of England and the British and Foreign Schools' Society was non-denominational. In 1823, Staines had three such schools, the National school

1801	1,750
1821	1,957
1831	2,486
1841	2,487
1851	2,577
1861	2,794
1871	3,659
1881	4,638
1891	5,060
1898	c. 6,000

84 Population growth in Staines during the 19th century. (All figures are taken from directories.)

for boys having 120 places and a curriculum consisting of 'etymology, grammar and the higher parts of arithmetic'. By 1850, this school was situated in London Road and had 247 places. In Bridge Street there was a National school for girls (128 places) and an infants department (148 places). The British school was in Thames Street and provided for boys (150), girls (110) and infants (120 places).

From the 1830s, there was a school of industry in Church Street. Its purpose was to provide a practical, technical kind of education for poor children who might otherwise have been in trouble and without work. It was a charity school entirely dependent on one benefactor, Miss Margaret Pope. She was described as 'a most benevolent lady whose liberality is not confined to any one particular class or locality'. In early life Miss Pope had had some experience of teaching in the British and Foreign school. She was a member of a leading medical family in the area; her father Robert had a practice in Staines in partnership with William Tothill and he was also physician to George III.

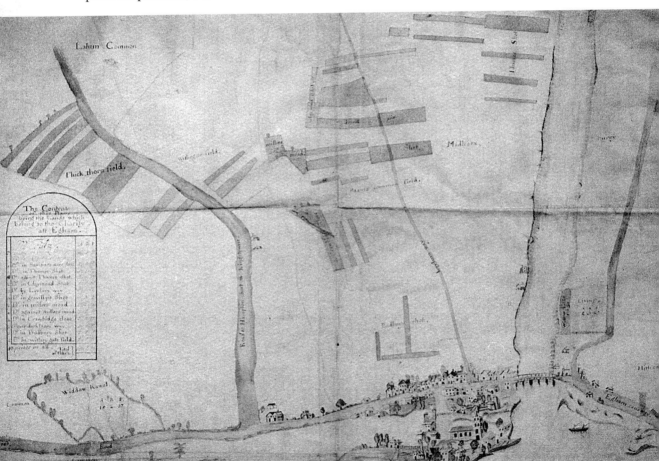

85   Plan by John Dugleby, 1798, highlighting the holdings of the Coopers' Company which it held as trustee of Strode's charity. North is at the bottom of the plan. Staines field occupies the centre; Thick Thorn field is to the left of the Kingston Road. On the far right are the River Thames and the road to Chertsey. (Copyright of Surrey History Service.)

86 Staines High Street and the junction with Clarence Street, *c.*1910. The fine façades belong to well-established family businesses.

Both Tothill and Pope were Quakers, as, of course, was Margaret. On her death she left money to endow a new school.

Dissent was long and well established. In the 17th century Quakers and Presbyterians defied persecution and grew to be a substantial proportion of townspeople. The Quakers acquired land on the High Street in 1840 and built a new meeting house with a burial ground to the rear. Their former burial ground behind Church Street on land given by Thomas Finch in 1765 had become too small. In the early 1830s the Congregationalists built a new classical-style church in Thames Street and the Baptists built one in Bridge Street.

The parish church of St Mary's was also rebuilt as a result of its fabric becoming so neglected and dilapidated that part of the north transept – a window and 16 feet of

wall – collapsed during a storm in 1827. Only the tower (1631) was left in the rebuilding of a larger church to accommodate about 1,000 people. The tower was heightened at the same time so that only the two lower stages remain of the 1631 structure. The living remained in the presentation of the Crown and, later, the Lord Chancellor. It was worth £200, and was enhanced to £492 by adding responsibility for perpetual curacies at Ashford and Laleham. The vicar was entitled to the lesser tithe but three impropriators, Coussmaker, Hartwell and Irving, had possession of the greater tithe. Their predecessors had been unsuccessfully challenged in the 1750s by the churchwardens in a long-drawn-out court case.

The coming of the railway in 1848 marked the beginning of a period of huge change. The impact was slow in being felt but

87 'River Thames', a painting by William Knight, 1859, looking downstream from Staines Bridge.

it proved decisive. The London and South-Western Railway Company built Staines' first railway link and Staines was a mere incidental station between Richmond and the company's objective, which was Windsor. It seems that initially the railway was viewed with suspicion and was certainly given only a passing, indirect mention in local directories. In 1852, Kelly's *Directory* mentioned the existence of a *Railway Hotel* at Knowle Green, hard by the station (which was not mentioned) and then stated that the Great Western Railway was at Slough. It took several attempts in the following eight years to extend a line from Staines westward to Wokingham and Reading, where the GWR had had a station since 1839. Objections to the proposed extension included fears that the railway would bring 'crowds of the commonest description' from London and Mr Edgell's complaint that it would ruin the view of ornamental trees from his Egham home, Milton Place. After several attempts, an Act of Parliament was passed in 1853 allowing the Staines, Wokingham and Woking Railway Company the legal powers to construct the westward continuation. In Egham, the church bells were rung at the news. One of the main commercial arguments for the line was the volume of

traffic that the Ascot races would generate. Once again, bridging the Thames proved an engineering challenge to create sound foundations. The aesthetic challenge was not even considered. The work was completed in May 1856 and a small spur was built west of Staines to connect the Wokingham line with the Windsor line. The two railway companies, the London and South-Western and the Staines, Wokingham and Woking amalgamated in 1878.

The railway changed the appearance of Staines most obviously with the bridge over the Thames and the viaduct from the station at Knowle Green (later called Staines Junction) over the High Street near the junction with Kingston Road. The population grew at a faster rate from the 1860s, reaching 6,500 by the end of the 19th century. In part this was due to a decline in infant mortality, but in part it was also because of an inflow of new families coming to find work in new and expanding industries. The latter were attracted by the improved communications. Existing enterprises recognised that wider markets would support their expansion. The result was the spread of new housing, at first near the station and later off the Kingston Road and south of Thames Street towards Laleham.

Chapter Ten

INTO THE TWENTIETH CENTURY

The diversification and expansion of industry was the most obvious and influential result of the arrival of the railway in Staines. Existing enterprises had scope to develop as markets opened up to them. As early as the 1820s, the Finch family had added mustard-milling to their flour-milling business and went into partnership with James Rickman. By mid-century they were still a major industry in the town and in the 1860s they had a London office in Upper Thames Street. The Ashby family had diversified even earlier when the founder of the family business established a bank in 1796 and took over the Middlesex and Surrey Bank in 1801. Thomas Ashby's sons developed the brewery, which, by 1846, was described as standing 'very prominent' and providing 'constant employment to a great number of workmen'. When the brewery was rebuilt in 1903, its tower (still there) dominated the town. In 1931, Ashby's was taken over by the Reading brewers, H. & G. Simmonds, together with over 100 public houses. Later it was swallowed up in the great expansion of Courage. Brewing in Staines ended in 1950 although bottling continued for some years.

A new industry came to Hale Mill, leased from Finch's in the 1850s. This was the Patent Wood or Fibrous Slab Company run by Walter Clare. The product was more familiarly known as papier-mâché and was popular for a wide range of furniture and decorative objects. The Staines factory exported some of its output to Australia for building houses. Several other smaller enterprises developed in the town, taking advantage of better transport and access to a wide market. In the 1860s, a domestic industry of making candles, originally a farming family's sideline, became a familiar but evil-smelling feature at the junction of the London and Kingston roads.

From 1860, the river traffic declined as the railway became more popularly accepted. With the decline in income, the wages of lock-keepers were cut. A contemporary change in river authority and management was the surrender of its claim of jurisdiction over the Thames by the City of London and the establishment, in 1856, of the Thames Conservancy Board. Heavy goods, such as coal and timber, continued to move by river and some of this trade continued well into the 20th century. However, there was a shift away from the river wharves by coal, corn and timber merchants to set up yards next to the railway station. Conveniently, nearby was Harris' brewery and Hodder's, who made Windsor sauce. These numerous small and medium-scale employers eventually had an impact on the townscape as new streets were laid out and artisan cottages built off the London and Kingston roads. Development at and all around Pound mill also contributed hugely to these changes. An engineer and inventor from Manchester, Frederick Walton, took a lease on Hale Mill, in 1864, apparently because it had large rollers originally used in the production of calico. Walton's invention was the cheap and cheerful floor covering called linoleum. It was made from a mixture of linseed, resin and crushed cork all pressed into a hessian backing. The venture proved very successful. Walton's company bought the Hale Mill in 1871 and extended its activities to the Pound Mill and the railway. The product was bulky and large storage spaces were required for the raw materials and the finished linoleum. Eventually the linoleum company occupied a site of 20 acres and became one of the largest employers in Staines. Some idea of its scale comes from David Barker's First World War statistics: 673

linoleum workers joined the armed forces, of whom 83 were killed.

Popular services developed to cater for the varied needs of the growing population of workers. Inns and beer retailers were numerous: there were seldom fewer than a dozen of the former and in 1852 there were seven of the latter. For those who sought self-improvement through education there was the Mechanics' Institute in Church Street, two reading rooms, one linked to the library and one associated with Miss Jane Norris's bookshop. There had been a circulating library since at least 1823 but it probably was patronised mainly by the middle and leisured classes. There were also schemes to encourage self-help and thrift. The savings bank, run from an office in Church Street, was under the supervision of the District

88   Oast house, now used as an adult education centre, but a reminder of the brewing industry. This was the site of Harris' Brewery.

Attorney, Mr James Mitchener being its secretary. It opened on Mondays from noon until 2 p.m. presumably to attract deposits as soon as possible after Saturday payday. These were the days of a long working week, which included Saturday mornings.

In the 1870s, the West Middlesex Building Society had an office in Clarence Street. It was part of a nationwide movement to encourage saving and home ownership, offering loans at reasonable rates of interest and, since the societies were mutual enterprises, investors were members of the societies rather than subjects of middle-class patronage. Another self-help scheme was the Co-operative movement, tempering uncontrolled capitalism and protecting consumers. It came somewhat late to Staines – the first co-operatives had their origin in the 1840s in Lancashire – and appeared in 1882 as the Staines and Egham Industrial Co-operative Society. It was so successful at its Kingston Road store that it soon expanded not only its site but also the scope of its operation. It set an example of good employment and honest trading.

The churches were also keen to be in the forefront of attempts at improving social and personal morality. The key to success was first providing more pews for the expanding population. The parish church expanded by building a mission church on Engell Road, where new housing had developed. In 1885, it was improved and provided 400 seats. It was designated as a chapel of ease, dedicated to St Peter and within the parish of St Mary's. In 1893, this rather undistinguished building found a benefactor in Sir Edward Clarke, Q.C., the Solicitor-General. He had come to live nearby in Staines and worshipped at St Peter's. His generosity provided the land on the Laleham Road to build a fine new St Peter's constructed of 'prosperous brick' (according to Pevsner) and with an interior that features iron and brass fretwork and windows stained pink, blue and mauve. The steeple enhances the downstream view along the river from the bridges.

A new Wesleyan church was built in 1890 in Kingston Road, another area with new housing. Meeting a need in a less traditional way was the Mission Hall in Hale Street

89   Old linoleum works, 1989, being viewed by a local industrial archaeology group.

(non-denominational) and the Salvation Army.

Civic awareness and identity found expression in transforming the old town centre. Since the 17th century there had been a covered market hall at the approach to the old bridge. The area had been rather by-passed and neglected since the construction of the new bridge and the opening of Clarence Street as its approach. Clearing the old market and erecting a substantial, four-square but lofty town hall of white brick and stone dressing restored the central focus of the town and gave it a new sense of dignity. Civic awareness was further encouraged by the local publication of two newspapers, *The West Middlesex Times* and *The Middlesex and Surrey Express*.

In other ways, a more modern town was being created. Hitherto local government had been in the hands of the parish vestry and, decreasingly, the manorial court. The

latter was totally out-dated and the former increasingly inadequate and unrepresentative of a community where dissent flourished and the Anglican parish organisation was irrelevant. New responsibilities were undertaken in the course of the 19th century by single-purpose boards, elected on a restricted property basis. This method of developing local government was initiated by the administrative arrangements of the New Poor Law. A union of 12 parishes, headed by Staines, was set up in 1836. Much later a school board to oversee elementary education and to supplement the contribution of the church societies came into being in 1885. As a framework for more modern and inclusive local government, Staines adopted the urban authority form, also in 1885. It became the uniform unit of local government, alongside rural districts, under the terms of the 1888 Act, which set up county councils. The first Staines Urban District Council had 12

90   St Peter's Church, *c.*1906, from the river. It was the gift of Sir Edward and Lady Clarke.

91   Interior of St Peter's Church. (Copyright of Surrey History Service.)

elected councillors who chose John Ashby, the last Staines resident of the dynasty, as its chairman.

Staines took its time in coming to grips with universal elementary education and it was not until 1896 that a school board was set up to make provision where the religious schools societies had not already made available sufficient school places. Wyatt Road School was the first 'board' school, followed by Kingston Road and Stanwell Road schools. All three were governed by one board of managers on which six Middlesex County Councillors and three Staines Urban District Councillors served. The evidence of their minutes for the 1920s and 1930s suggests that their governance was remarkably detailed by today's standards. The meetings were monthly in term-time. The chairman signed requisitions for stationery, approved the annual change of timetable for the four days of Ascot week so that the children avoided the race traffic, which all passed through the High Street, and signed the school logbooks monthly. Even a rare school outing of a very serious educational nature, to Richmond, to hear lectures about the products of the Empire, was reported in minute detail to the board.

The financial regime under which the schools were run was never generous; corners were cut, repairs delayed (perhaps more a result of incompetence than economy) and staffing levels were unbelievably tough. At Wyatt Road School, which had infants and juniors, there were five classes in 1928 totalling 246 pupils; one had 35 children, the other four 50 or more. When the future of Stanwell Road School was uncertain the headmistress was not replaced and a young uncertificated teacher was drafted in to 'help out'. When the ageing

92 Staines High Street, *c*.1904, showing the large gaslights hanging over the shop windows.

buildings needed maintenance, the response was slow. Stanwell reported temperatures averaging each day from 46°F to 52°F during November and December 1929. The managers ordered five 'tortoise' stores in March 1930. However, small amounts of comfort were permitted. One lounge chair was ordered for the staff room at Wyatt Road and Staines, lino was laid in the two staff rooms (one for women, one for men) at Kingston Road School.

The curriculum received little attention; no such phrase as 'development' passed the pen of the minuting secretary. The one sign of development was noted in 1928 when an application for a laboratory demonstration table was approved. This would enable general science to be taught, by demonstration, to senior scholars. It followed a report by visiting members of His Majesty's Inspectorate.

Children were able to leave school at 13 years of age and thereafter a number attended evening classes, which also came within the managers' supervision. During the 1920s and 1930s, the numbers attending were between 150 and 200, with some pupils following more than one subject. Technical and vocational subjects were taught: typewriting, shorthand, bookkeeping, commercial arithmetic, applied mechanics, mathematics, commercial correspondence, machine construction and building construction constituted the curriculum. In the late 1930s, French was added. The management costs of the whole operation were a little under £450 a year, the teachers receiving 7s. an hour. Those scholars with a good attendance record (over 80 per cent), were approved for free tuition. The only other route for improvement was open to those who could afford to pay fees for grammar school (at Strode's in Egham for boys) or who gained a free place by winning a competitive county council 'scholarship'. These were few and for the whole of West Middlesex only 19 or 20 were awarded annually.

Staff were poorly paid and women were doubly discriminated against. Their salaries were on a lower scale than men's salaries, for the same work, and they had to resign on marriage. In 1936, the Middlesex Education Committee issued a new recommendation, that married women could be employed and that it was often beneficial that they be on the staff of schools. Staines managers were unmoved until, in the experiences of war, they agreed to re-employ a teacher who had married but only on a temporary contract that would cease with hostilities.

There were times of relaxation and fun to lighten the harshness of much of the work for both children and teachers. Empire Day was celebrated each year in Staines as part of the carnival and fundraising for charity. It merited a holiday. A half-holiday was granted for the county rugby championships at Twickenham and a whole day for Prince George, later the Duke of Kent, on his marriage to Princess Marina of Greece. The local education authority paid for swimming lessons for 10 weeks in summer for senior scholars. These took place in the river with a raft and punt as safety measures. Welfare provision reached many children through school. From January 1933, free daily milk was provided for needy, malnourished children and made available to all at 1d. a day. In 1935, facilities were provided at Stanwell Road School for children to eat a packed lunch if they had a walk from home of more than one-and-a-half miles. Otherwise, children went home at midday for their meal, almost two hours being allowed for the break. There were also regular medical inspections and for this purpose a prefabricated hut was provided at Kingston Road School, where

93 The Square and town hall. From the 1880s the new town hall created a focus in an area that had been bypassed when the bridge was moved upstream.

94   Staines town hall from the river.

increasing numbers put pressure on space in the main building.

Early in 1933, discussion began about a new school building. There was some urgency because so much suitable land was being earmarked for housing. In September 1936, the site was chosen on the area known as the Laleham House estate. Building began, but war broke out and progress was held up. The urgency was a combination of increasing numbers in what had become a senior division at Kingston Road School and the proposal to raise the school leaving age. On the eve of war, the school had 196 boys and 163 girls organised into one department and providing the vestiges of secondary education. The need for a new elementary school to replace the Stanwell and Wyatt schools was recognised and two sites were identified, on Long Lane, Stanwell and near Stanwell Road, Ashford. It would cater for either 800 or 900 children. The outbreak of war suspended all these projects.

In a final flourish of railway construction, the Staines & West Drayton Railway Company was formed to link Staines to the Great Western line. Work began in 1885 across Staines Moor to Poyle and Colnbrook. Its terminus station in Staines was Moor House, until 1849 the home of Charles Finch. This became Staines West Station. It was the town's third. A year earlier Staines High Street Station was opened near the *Garibaldi Inn*. This station was closed in 1916. In 1895, another station was opened on the West Drayton line to serve the rifle ranges on the moor. It was at first called Runemede Range and later Yeoveney Halt.

There were two ranges on the moor. The War Office closed the earlier one, in use from 1862 to 1892 by the 44th Middlesex Rifle Volunteer Corps, after complaints from the railway company, fearing for the safety of its passengers. Subsequently, more extensive ranges were then created for the Metropolitan Rifle Range Company. These were claimed to be the largest firing practice ground in the world, with 70 targets covering an area two-and-a-half miles in length by one-and-a-half in breadth. The project flourished until the years following the First World War, declining from about 1920 and then being closed in 1930. An area known as the Butts survives in the northern part of the moor, where a mound remains looking more like a prehistoric earthwork than an aid to 20th-century warfare.

Speedier and cheaper communications by rail and the shortening of working hours contributed to the development of many leisure activities that were enjoyed throughout the different social classes. In the past, leisure had been the privilege of the wealthiest and then of the middle class but by the late 19th century ordinary working folk could afford to relax. The river became an important focus for the growth in leisure activities. Boat builders, who were often also hirers of boats, skiffs and punts, became a feature of the Staines riverside. Biffens operated from the Surrey bank and Tims began on the Middlesex bank by Church

95   Staines' old post office, one of three stylish buildings all now demolished.

96 Penton Hook on the southern edge of the parish gained a reputation for unruly behaviour. The riverside bungalows were a sign that people had more leisure time to enjoy the recreational activities of the river.

Island before moving across to their site just below the railway bridge. Pleasure boating soon led to the creation of boating clubs – the Philhurst in Gresham Road, Staines Boat Club upstream from the railway bridge – and, in turn, these clubs promoted regattas. The Staines and Egham Junior Regatta ran from 1906 to 1931. The Staines Amateur Regatta began in 1850, one year before the founding of the Staines Boat Club. This regatta was the first one, after Henley, to race eights. For professionals there was the Staines and Egham Watermen. The use of the Church Lammas for picnics and bathing continued into the 20th century and was encouraged by the gift to the town of 15½ acres by John Ashby in 1922. The impression of a riverside resort was promoted by the development of small bungalows, many on Church Island and on the Surrey bank.

In the early 20th century, Staines benefited from the diversification of its industry into light engineering and services. The Manor Place works of W.E. Sykes had begun producing machine tools in Egham in 1927 and moved to its Staines site alongside the railway in 1935. The firm had a widespread reputation for precision gear-cutting and at the height of its success employed close on 1,000 workers. Another example of engineering in Staines was the company set up in 1905 by Harry H. Gardam on land purchased from Ashby's brewery. The Middlesex and Surrey Laundry in London Road employed around 500 in the inter-war years. The laundry was one of the first to be purpose-built. Like the breweries, it relied for its water supply on artesian wells. Across the river, on the site now occupied by Sainsbury's, the Lagonda works produced luxury cars. The origin, in 1904, was humble enough: a small site in Thorpe Road making motorcycles. In 1947 it was taken over by Aston Martin, and Petters Limited, engine manufacturers, acquired the site. Lacking older, staple industries, Staines did not experience the full impact of the 1930s depression in trade. Employment in 'newer' industries remained buoyant. Testimony to the prosperity of the time are the residential roads to the south and south-east of the town centre where aspiring home-owners realised their dreams of a 'semi' and garden in an Avenue, Crescent, Grove or Gardens. Several hundred new houses built speculatively in the early 1930s sold quickly.

The building boom was not restricted to housing. The appearance of the High Street took on the form many older inhabitants recall from the immediate post-war years. The most notable changes were the multiple stores that came into the town in the 1930s. W.H. Smith arrived in 1934 and Marks & Spencer in 1935. At the junction of Church Street and the High Street there was a market building that became the first local site for Tesco. It stood somewhat incongruously between the 17th-century cottages of Church Street and the site of the old *George Inn*, which had been demolished. When redevelopment took place in 1959, Tesco eventually moved out of town and a modern *George Inn* was built on the old site. By the time war broke out pressure was already building up to improve, in some way, the town centre. The growth of motorised traffic alongside the survival of some horse and cart delivery tended to cause conflict between vehicular and pedestrian traffic. The solution was hard to find and, in any case, had to be abandoned before the exclusive demands of war.

The immediate environs of Staines changed radically during the 20th century. The first major change, consequent on the setting up in 1902 of the Metropolitan Water Board and more coherent planning for the future supply of water, was the excavation

97 *Bridge House Hotel* was originally Bridge House, built in 1832 by the Staines attorney, Randolph Horne, who was also clerk to the Bridge Commissioners. (Copyright of Surrey History Service.)

98 *Swan Hotel*, drawing room *c.*1900, advertising the comfort of a leisure break in Staines.

99 Church Eyot showing the boat-building business of Tims before they moved across the river. (Copyright of Surrey History Service.)

100   The Watermen's regatta. (Copyright of Surrey History Service.)

of a pair of huge reservoirs north of the A30. The period of excavation brought mixed blessings. The navvies employed on the scheme gave the area a bad reputation and the general disruption and dirt depressed property values. But for landowners, for example the trustees of Strode's charity in Egham, it brought handsome compensation. It also stimulated the development of property at the eastern (London Road) end of the town. The visual impact was huge. In such a flat, featureless landscape, there was no concealing the intrusion. Instead, the high embankments of the reservoirs were laid to pasture where grazing sheep introduce a slightly surreal air of calm downland beneath the Heathrow flight paths.

Remarkably, being only 17 miles from central London, Staines town centre suffered very little from bombing. The appearance of the High Street in the late 1950s differed little from that of the 1930s. Defensive measures naturally focused on the bridge, where preparations were made at each end to take tank traps. The Scientific and Literacy Institute on the corner of Clarence Street and Bridge Street became a defence post. As a further precaution in case the bridge was damaged or destroyed by bombs, a temporary structure, the Callender-Hamilton bridge, was constructed in 1941 and survived until 1947. After that, until completely removed in 1959, it was a pedestrian bridge. Mobile ack-ack guns were mounted on railway trucks to run parallel to the causeway. Even the scale of modern warfare had not obliterated the strategic importance of sites that had existed for a millennium.

The reservoirs were brought into a new kind of use. The twin ones provided a site suitable for practising bouncing bombs prior to the dambuster raids. The George VI reservoir, simply designated the 'new' reservoir, had progressed well from its inception in 1937 until the outbreak of war in 1939. Major building work almost ceased because the heavy plant, much of it imported from America, was requisitioned for the war

101 Bell Weir lock on a busy day, demonstrating the popularity of the river for recreation. The lock and its accompanying weir span the river at a wide point but where a gravel bank made possible the construction of the lock in 1817. It was named after its first lock-keeper, Charles Bell.

effort. However, the area proved useful for testing flamethrowers and for developing methods of dispersing fog to allow aircraft to land safely. (These were very early days for radar.) There is also a tradition that the reservoir was used to construct a model of Clapham Junction as a decoy for German bombers. Another version substitutes the HMV factory at Bedfont. These pieces of folklore have no official corroboration. However, these sites may well, in themselves, have decoyed enemy bombers from central Staines. The vast majority of bombs fell on the moor and Lammas. The worst civilian casualties were in Stainash Crescent, where four people were killed and 17 injured.

As in the rest of the country, Staines' industrial activity was transformed to support the war effort. One of the more remarkable examples was the revival of traditional basket-making, always an important local industry fed by the osier beds along the Thames. F. Lewis, whose shop was in the High Street, supplied baskets as containers for medical supplies for the Forces. They were used in the Arnhem parachute attack. The larger factories, including Lagonda, Perrings and the Linoleum works, were diverted to military supplies. Lagonda made munitions, Hoover, in the Perring works, made wiring for aircraft and the Linoleum works made torpedoes.

Chapter Eleven

RECENT TIMES

In 1945 there was relief and rejoicing as first the war in Europe and then, three months later in August, the Far East came to an end. Staines had good reason for relief. Remarkably, although only 17 miles from Hyde Park Corner, the town centre had escaped with little bomb damage. After the celebrations and victory parades that filled the streets, the next occasion for a little glamour and excitement to lift spirits above the post-war gloom of continued (and even more restrictive) food rationing, shortages of housing and consumer goods was the opening of a new reservoir by the King and Queen. This took place on 7 November 1947, shortly before the wedding of Princess Elizabeth. Glamour might not have been the first thought of the specially invited guests when their invitation contained a recommendation to wear stout shoes and warm clothing.

The reservoir was named after King George VI. Its construction had been authorised by an Act of Parliament in 1935 for the Metropolitan Water Board to meet the ever-expanding water requirements of London. During the war, work had been virtually suspended. Whereas between 700 and 1,000 men worked on the scheme between 1937 and 1939, the labour force was down to about 30 in 1944 with some help from German prisoners-of-war. It increased the capacity of water in the three reservoirs north of Staines by 130 per cent.

The town as well as individuals needed to pick up the threads dropped in 1939. Then one of the major requirements in Staines and even more in adjacent areas was the provision of new housing. Plans on the eve of war were for the development of Heathrow as a major international airport. Planning for this had begun before the war and there had already been a little new building. In the euphoric mood of 1945, new requirements were added to allow for the removal of sub-standard homes. The airport's need for housing new employees was estimated to be 3,300 homes. These were mainly to be built at Ashford, Feltham, Heston, Stanwell and Sunbury. Stanwell, for example, was to have 706 new homes. However, it became clear that more new homes would be needed in Staines, if not immediately for Heathrow workers then for the new industries that the airport's expansion would generate. By 1947, in response to the government's house-building programme, five sites were identified between Staines and Laleham: 700 off Commercial Road, 300 near the new Matthew Arnold Secondary schools and others off Worple Road and Ashford Road. The first group of road names betrayed the era of their construction: Elizabeth, Edinburgh and Charles Roads.

102 Staines reservoir completed, 1902. A view across one of the twin reservoirs constructed for the Metropolitan
Board of Works. Water was pumped along on an aqueduct from the River Thames at Bell Weir and thence from
the reservoir to Hampton.

The war had curtailed what became the inexorable growth of motorised traffic, but by the end of the 1950s the town came near to strangulation by cars and lorries, most of them through-traffic. It seemed that Staines' historic strategic site, where the Great South-West road crossed the Thames, was becoming more a burden than an asset.

Two simultaneous solutions were sought to the traffic problem. One was internal: to make it easier for local traffic to circulate. The other was to provide a by-pass to take through-traffic out of the town. The first of these solutions can, with hindsight, be regretted as short-sighted vandalism. The configuration of old street patterns, narrow junctions and awkwardly sited ancient buildings was sacrificed to 'improvement'. The result was an increase in traffic to fill the new spaces that the bulldozer provided.

In spite of being granted listed-building status in 1953 the *White Lion*, dating from

the 16th century, was demolished in order to widen a narrow section of the High Street near the railway bridge. The narrow and awkward junction of Thames Street and the High Street was for decades a project for widening. After 1914, a scheme was shelved because of the cost of purchasing property. Eventually the destroy-and-build mentality of the 1950s succeeded in sweeping away the old shops, family-run and specialist, to be replaced on new alignments by department stores. One of Staines' very few modestly distinguished buildings, the 1837 classical-style congregational chapel, was swept away in this redevelopment to make way for the traffic. The second prong of the attack on traffic congestion was the construction of the A30 by-pass to the north. In 1961, the first phase was opened to carry traffic heading to or from London. Traffic for Kingston, using the A308, still needed to go through the town until the second phase of the by-pass was built from the *Crooked Billet* towards Ashford.

As well as needing to provide more homes after the war, there was a need for more school accommodation. The 1944 Education Act, which aimed at the provision of secondary education, whether general (and modern) or technical or academic, had also provided for the leaving age to be raised from 14 to 15. The secondary schools planned just before the war were completed and named the Matthew Arnold schools by 1954. Ten years later both were feeling the pressure of numbers with over 600 girls and 700 boys on their rolls. Numbers were

also high at the two Abbotsford schools in Ashford. All these schools faced a further raising of the school-leaving age and all aspired to provide sixth-form education. The rapid growth of Stanwell, which had no secondary schools, was another cause of pressure.

The fifth school that made up the original group of schools all managed by the same governing body was Ashford County School. It had over 800 pupils and a sixth form. Because the fledgling sixth forms in the four secondary schools could offer a very small range of subjects, particularly true of the two girls' schools, there was some

103   Staines Bridge, *c.*1949, showing the Callender-Hamilton bridge which became an early post-war relief road for pedestrians across the river.

transfer of pupils to the Ashford sixth form. In 1967, Matthew Arnold Girls School could not offer physics, mathematics or English literature at 'A' level. It was an extravagant form of teaching to have as few as six 'A'-level candidates.

The frustrations as well as the achievements of the schools were well illustrated in the coded language of official papers. Occasionally real anger breaks through, as when one of the schools resorted to paying pupils to clear the new playing fields of stones and flints so that they could be rolled and seeded. Extra portable classrooms, laughingly called temporary accommodation, arrived late and well after the start of the school year when a whole extra year group had to be housed. When a new school was built in Stanwell to ease the pressures in Ashford and Staines, its planned opening had to be delayed until 1970. Even then, it opened unfinished. This was hardly a tribute to the efficiency and effectiveness of local administration. However, it was a culture to which teachers became inured and, in spite of everything, they provided new courses. The Certificate

104   The Lagonda car works on the Causeway.

105   Lagonda model, 1921.

of Secondary Education was introduced alongside 'O' levels, and Royal Society of Arts examinations, mainly in secretarial and office practice, were provided, particularly in the girls' schools. Work experience, links with local businesses, careers outings, field trips and holidays abroad as well as fundraising for a new hall, for charities and the introduction of the Duke of Edinburgh Award Scheme all illustrate the breadth of the education that was provided. Much of it was in 'after hours' time, given by staff. Sometimes it happened in spite of leaking roofs – it took seven years to cure one – and in spite of the heating breaking down for several weeks and dangerous, open trenches being left for several more.

In addition to huge and continuing changes to the school curriculum, with the accompanying requirements for teachers to upgrade and develop their skills and knowledge, there were fundamental changes being planned for the whole structure of secondary education. Local Education Authorities had been required by a circular in 1965, issued by Shirley Williams, Secretary of State for Education, to submit plans for reorganisation along comprehensive lines. Surrey took its time but eventually settled for a 'mixed economy', trying to match arrangements to the existing building stock of schools and the prejudices of vocal parents and politicians. Some areas of the county retained schools with sixth forms where the latter were well developed; others, including Spelthorne, were to become 12-16 secondary schools, lose any embryonic sixth form and have two sixth-form colleges to provide the breadth and choice of curriculum that it was difficult for a school to provide. Ashford

106 Aerial view of Staines, 1936, with the Lagonda works in the foreground; the Ashby brewery, left across the river; and to its right the large complex of the linoleum works now occupied by the Two Rivers shopping area.

County School was selected as the college for the Staines area, intended to cater for 600 students while the Sunbury area was to have a college of similar size. In the run-up to this reorganisation, the two Matthew Arnold schools and the Abbotsford pair were amalgamated, each under a headmaster, and the age of transfer from primary schools was raised from 11 to 12 plus. In keeping with tradition, none of the promised alterations had taken place at Ashford in time for its

opening, in 1975, as a sixth-form college. Change did not seem to have solved many problems; rather it raised new ones that, in the fashion of the times, were called challenges.

Other challenges had to be faced arising from a growing public awareness of environmental issues. The changes brought about by the building of the A30 by-pass and road-widening in Thames Street and the High Street gave only temporary relief from the difficulties of congestion and the dangerous entanglement of vehicular and pedestrian traffic. These matters rested in the 1960s, a decade now seen as one of insouciant neglect and environmental damage and disregard for the fragility of social structures. These attitudes were hard to dispel ten years on, particularly when the economy was seriously faltering. It was easy to dismiss campaigns to preserve the past, whether buildings, townscapes or patches of countryside, as uneconomic. In Staines, the 1970s began with alarm that gravel-digging was threatened on the moor. Other pressures came from the inexorable build-up of traffic congestion and lack of car parking in the town centre and from an imminent shake-up in local government every bit as radical as the creation of county and district councils at the end of the 19th century.

The outcome of the Royal Commission on local government reform, set up by Richard Crossman and chaired by Lord Redcliffe-Maud, was a radical reform. Locally it meant that the Staines Urban District Council was abolished and a new unit, which included Sunbury, became the borough of Spelthorne, thus reviving the name of one of the Hundreds of Middlesex and making an appeal to the past in order to gain support for innovation. Interestingly, it was also decided to have no second-tier parish or town councils. For this reason, the new borough was given a good chance to establish its identity and encourage a sense of civic loyalty and pride. Civic leaders must have felt a small degree of vindication when, as a result of the publication of the 1991 census, people's sense of belonging to the new borough was tested. Only nine per cent declared they had no sense of belonging; Hounslow's figure was 76 per cent. The results of the survey of local loyalty were as follows:

Degree of sense of belonging	% of population of Spelthorne
A great deal	23
A fair amount	48
A little	20
Not at all	9

In parallel with this change, there was a spate of building that was greatly needed. For decades, the town hall had been inadequate for the needs of mid-20th-century local government. Several departments moved out into other accommodation in Clarence Street, London Road and, from 1952, Elmsleigh House, later the site of massive redevelopment. Planning for a new civic centre began in the 1930s (according to J.L. and David M. Barker in *Snapshots of Staines*). Only in the 1970s was the reality achieved at Knowle Green where a new civic centre gradually came to fruition. The first building to be opened in 1972 was that of the new council offices, which brought together all the departments and offices scattered about the town. In 1976, new magistrates' courts were completed at Knowle Green to a design by the Surrey County architect. These served the petty sessions of Staines and Sunbury and they were designed to keep separate all the varied groups of people who should not mix in the setting of law courts. The design also paid particular attention to acoustics within the court and soundproofing against the traffic outside.

The first attempt to improve the flow of traffic and ease congestion within the town centre was only partially successful. It focused on the key idea of creating a pedestrian zone along the High Street to make conditions not only safer but also more pleasant for shoppers. Maintaining and improving Staines' appeal as a major retail centre underlaid many of the planning schemes of the post-war years. This aim was entirely understandable as some of the town's largest engineering firms closed or withdrew. W.E. Sykes had, for example, ceased their large operation at Manor Place. Retailing was, therefore, regarded as increasingly important to maintain employment levels and to boost the local economy. In the early 1970s, the first phase of the town centre improvement plan was completed with the construction of a southern route to by-pass the High Street from its junction with Kingston Road round to the junction with Thames Street. Associated with the new south road were a new library and a bus station. The second crucial phase to the north of the High Street (the present Mustard Mill Road) was a victim of national was well as local government cut-backs in spending during the economic crisis of the early 1970s. This encompassed the three-day

week, major strikes, high-level inflation and the 1973 Middle East war that led to an oil shortage. In such circumstances, 'expensive' road schemes were judged unaffordable and, as a consequence, Staines did not get its long-planned pedestrian High Street.

One consequence was to put into action a compromise plan to ease the traffic problem and this was made possible by the existence of the new South Street. The High Street became one-way from the junction of Thames Street to the junction with Kingston Road, from where South Street took all the town-centre traffic flowing westwards towards the bridge. These arrangements continued until the big push towards the millennium when the northern route across the site of the linoleum works completed the scheme first planned more than 30 years earlier.

Meanwhile, closely related to these events was the growth of concern about the damage

107 Runnymede Rifle Ranges were developed after 1891 and followed the range set up by the 44th Middlesex Rifle Volunteer Corps. They were one of the largest ranges in Europe, until sold in 1920.

that development was inflicting on the urban landscape. The speed of change and its extent at last alerted 'the authorities' as well as citizens. One expression of this concern was the listing of buildings of architectural and historic interest. Obvious ones were the bridge, the town hall and St Mary's Church. In addition to a group of houses in Church Street and Market Square, the *Blue Anchor*, the Malthouse and Staines West Station were included. The next stage was to ensure that the context of the majority of the buildings was secure against out-of-character alterations, demolition and unsuitable new development. A designated conservation area was proposed in 1978 to achieve this end but no extension was subsequently allowed because no adjoining areas were judged to be of 'special architectural or historical interest'. Further measures were taken to protect the bridge by imposing a weight limit of 10 tons. Local pride in the town's most famous feature had been aroused by the knowledge that, during the war, the bridge had supported five stationary Churchill tanks totalling 120 tons.

Beyond the town and separated from it, after 1964, by the A30 by-pass was the ancient manor of Yeoveney and Staines Moor. From the evidence of surveys in the late 1950s, it was clear that this area had at least two archaeological sites. Plans for yet another reservoir and the demand of the construction industry for gravel (this was the era of the first motorways) placed this area under immediate threat. An Iron-Age enclosure was partly excavated on the moor and, at Yeoveney, adjacent to what became junction 13 on the M25, a Neolithic causeway camp or enclosure was discovered. A new landowner curtailed the excavation of the former; the latter was excavated and then destroyed by the reservoir, gravel-digging and motorway construction. The episodes were a call to arms for conservationists. The fears proved to be well founded when application was made for more gravel-digging on the moor. Superficially, it appeared that the moor was already well protected. It was part of the metropolitan green belt and within a regional park, the Colne Valley. Further, it was a site of Special Scientific Interest, protected since 1955 and, since 1866, protected from inclosure by the Metropolitan Commons Act. Ownership, however, remained with the lord of the manor. In recent times, the holders of this office have included the chairman of Taylor Woodrow and Stephen Brett of Robert Brett & Sons Limited, both companies with more than a passing interest in the use of gravel.

In theory, the ancient right to graze animals on the moor was open to all commoners. Traditionally they were defined as those whose smoking chimney could be seen from the church and, in practice, they were those residents of Staines who claimed their rights. The Commons Registration Act introduced more appropriate regulation in 1965. It granted commoners' rights only to those who registered. It is an indication of widespread interest that over 200 people registered as commoners and in so doing were allowed to assign their grazing rights, known locally as farrens, to other registered commoners. Until 1793, these farrens had been unrestricted but were subsequently allocated as two cows and one horse. Mean numbers of grazing in 1969-78 were 30 horses and 134 cattle and in 1981-88, 51 horses and 114 cows. New life was breathed into the moor's management. The Court Leet was the ancient body through which 12 moormasters were elected to control grazing and see to the proper maintenance of the moor and its fences. In addition, the local authority still held its responsibilities under late 19th-century legislation.

When, in 1971, a planning application to extract gravel was made by the Greenham Sand & Ballast Company and the Lady of the manor, the local authority rejected it. The applicants took the matter to appeal and a public inquiry was set in motion. A new organisation in Staines was set up as a consequence of this application and the controversy that it caused. This was the Association for the Preservation of Staines Moor (APSM). It achieved its immediate purpose when the secretary of state refused the planning application and took the opportunity to reinforce the importance and special status of the moor. Further attempts to secure permission to extract gravel from the moor were unsuccessful in 1977 and 1980.

As these local contests unfolded, the area behind the south side of the High Street was being cleared in preparation for an enclosed, covered shopping area, subsequently named Elmsleigh after the large house that was demolished. The 'Rescue' archaeology movement in the 1960s had successfully campaigned for the right to have an archaeological survey and, if necessary, a 'dig' to explore sites such as this one. The results of the Elmsleigh site were spectacular. They raised the status of Staines from a supposed but rather uncertain Roman site, its ancient reputation resting largely on the early 18th-century observations of William Stukeley in his *Iterarium Curiosum*, to that of the largest Roman settlement in Surrey. The Friends' Meeting House site and its burial ground proved particularly fruitful sources of Roman finds. The damp conditions near the river favoured the survival of artefacts and materials that normally perish. Hence Staines has examples of pieces of leather sandal that compete in interest with the much more extensive and famous site by the Roman wall at Vindolanda. The 'digs'

108   The Butts on Staines Moor – a surviving fragment of the Runnymede Ranges.

of the 1970s, the discovery, and loss, of the Yeoveney enclosure and the victory for preserving the moor were three events that were probably influential in encouraging a greater sense of civic pride. In turn, it seems that more people were prepared to become involved in preserving what remained of the past and was valuable.

The extent of participation in the evolution of the town's development plan between 1979 and 1983 was an expression of residents' desire to be involved and to give direction to public policy. The construction of the Elmsleigh Shopping Centre was the outcome of the key aim for the town as planning ideas had crystallised in the 1970s. That was to create a major retail centre for a wide area around Staines. As well as providing more shops (59 smaller units in all), there was provision for two large ones, British Home Stores and International Stores. There was a clearly stated policy of restricting non-retail outlets in the town centre. This, incidentally, marks a contrast with Egham, where no such determination existed among policy makers and where office spaces proliferated during the 1980s while retail shops disappeared. Staines avoided this competition between shops and offices, between retailers and service providers – banks, building societies and the rapidly growing offshoots of the computing industry. The Queen opened the Elmsleigh Shopping Centre in February 1980 after a little more than two years' construction. It was, of course, still only the first phase of what the planners and local leaders had originally hoped would be built.

A broad consultation exercise followed the publication of the town's draft plan in 1983. Individuals and groups responded in a way that showed a great deal of local concern and willingness to engage with local politicians and planners in working out solutions. Of course, there were powerful interest groups. The Elmsleigh traders were keen for the development of their neighbouring site, that of Johnson and Clark, to go ahead as a way of enhancing not just the approach to the Elmsleigh Shopping Centre but the totality of shopping facilities. Staines' substantial body of commuters wanted better provision for car parking at the station: the lack of space there seemingly virtually insoluble. Opinions on the provision of car parking differed. The 'green' lobby objected to the waste of space in planning extensive ground-level car parks. One such was at the riverside. The alternative was to add to the number of planned multi-storey ones. These carried higher costs not only in economic terms but also in less tangible ways, detracting from the appearance of the town. The congestion on the bridge proved

another topic of interest and controversy to residents. By the late 1970s it had become so endemic that there was some advocacy for its closure as soon as the construction of the link from the town's by-pass westwards was connected to the M25 at junction 13 and to the Runnymede Bridge, which continued the A30 route to Egham and the A308 to Windsor.

It took another decade before the inner road relief scheme was completed. This time the remnants of the linoleum factory were cleared and partly replaced by the Staines northern trading estate and, more recently, the Two Rivers shopping area with massive car parking space. Mustard Mill Road became the northern link from Hale Street to the junction with the High Street near the railway bridge and thence to South Street. All of this opened the way to a pedestrianised High Street. The completion of this work and the commissioning of art in the town centre to mark phases and events in Staines' history form a suitable commemoration of the millennium. They may also mark a belated reaction to the decades of destruction that, for too long, the townspeople of Staines were led to believe equated with progress.

Today Staines does not obviously reveal its past. Many of the features which might provide clues and visual evidence have disappeared: the important neolithic site at Yeoveney, the medieval church, the links with Westminster Abbey, the street pattern at the heart of the the old town and almost all the old buildings. Such losses are not all bad. They can result in the liberation of a community from too great a concern with the past, an attempt to hold on indiscriminately. A thriving community is one which sets its face towards the opportunities of the present day and the future. It is one which recognises that survival and growth imply change. That does not mean that knowing the town's history, caring for what survives and resisting wanton destruction does not have a key role to play. Staines is fortunate to have groups and individuals, dedicated and knowledgeable, who can celebrate its past and campaign vigorously to ensure that those vestiges of its history which remain are part of the future.

BIBLIOGRAPHY

rimary sources for the history of Staines can be found in the London Metropolitan
Archives, the Surrey History Centre and the National Archives. Staines is fortunate to
have a long run of churchwardens' and overseers' books. Unfortunately, throughout
the period of preparing this book, Staines' records in Staines were either totally unavailable
or were very limited of access. For the development of Nonconformity in the 17th century,
records held at Dr Williams Library, Gordon Square and Friends House, Euston Road have
been consulted. The diary of Henry Strode is in the Verney Archive at Claydon House.

Printed primary sources consulted included: Middlesex Sessions books ed. J.C. Jeaffreson;
Pickering's Statutes; Documents illustrating the rule of Walter de Wenlock, Abbot of
Westminster, 1283-1307 ed. B. Harvey; *Chertsey Abbey Cartularies* and *Chertsey Abbey
Court Rolls*, Surrey Record Society vol. 48 and vol XII, 1958 and 1963. Directories for Staines
(consulted with the kind permission of Ralph Parsons): *Universal British Directory*, 1798;
Pigot's *Directory*, 1823-24-1834; Robson's 1837; Hunt's 1846; Kelly's 1852, 1859 etc.

Robert Ashby, *Record of the Ashbys of Staines*, (1916)
J.L. & D.M. Barker, *Snapshots of Staines*
W. Beck and T.F. Ball, *London Friends' Meeting*, (1869)
Joseph Besse, *Suffering of the people called Quaker*, vol 1, (1740)
Margaret Bowker, *The Henrician Reformation*, (1981)
Eric Butterfield, *They Walked this Way* (1996)
Jonathan Cotton, Glenys Crocker, Audrey Graham eds., *Aspects of Archaeology and
     History in Surrey* (2004)
Jonathan Cotton and David Field eds., *Towards a new Stone Age* (2004)
The London and Middlesex Archaeological Society, New Series No. 27: *The Archaeology
     of Staines*, 1976
B. Harvey, *Westminster Abbey and its estates in the Middle Ages* (1977)

Secondary sources:
Revd Daniel Lysons, *County of Middlesex* (1980 reprint)
A.G. Matthews, *Calamy Revised* (1988)
Stuart P. Needham, *The Passage of the Thames*, vol 1 (2000)
Eric Pawson, *Trade, Transport and Economy* (1977)
Michael Robbins, *Middlesex* (1953, new edition, 2003)

R. Robertson-Mackay, *Excavations of the causewayed camp at Staines* (1962)

F.S. Thacker, *Thames Highway: General History* (1914); *Locks & Weirs,* (1920)

J. Thirsk ed., *Agrarian History of England & Wales*, vol viii (1978)

F. Turner, *Egham, A history of the Parish under Church and Crown* (1926)

Victoria County History of Middlesex, vol ii and vol iii (and in particular the essay on Staines by Susan Reynolds, 1961)

Victoria County History of Surrey, vols ii and iii

T.S. Willan, *River Navigation in England 1600-1750* (1936)

INDEX

Bold numbers indicate illustrations

Northern Staines, 1899